RECONCILIATION

S. Billie Mandle

KEHRER

Confession
Dorothy Day

When you go to confession on a Saturday night, you go into a warm, dimly lit vastness, with the smell of wax and incense in the air, the smell of burning candles, and if it is a hot summer night there is the sound of a great electric fan, and the noise of the streets coming in to emphasize the stillness.

—

Some confessionals are large and roomy—plenty of space for the knees, and breathing space in the thick darkness that seems to pulse with your own heart. In some poor churches, many of the ledges are narrow and

worn, so your knees almost slip off the kneeling bench, and your feet protrude outside the curtain which shields you from the others who are waiting. Some churches have netting, or screens, between you and priest and you can see the outline of his face inclined toward you, quiet, impersonal, patient. Some have a piece of material covering the screen, so you can see nothing.

"I have sinned. These are my sins." That is all you are supposed to tell; not the sins of others, or your own virtues, but only your ugly, gray, drab, monotonous sins.

1.

Saint Barbara
Saint Michael
Holy Cross
Saint Michael
Saint Thomas More
Saint Rocco
Visitation of the Virgin Mary
Most Holy Trinity

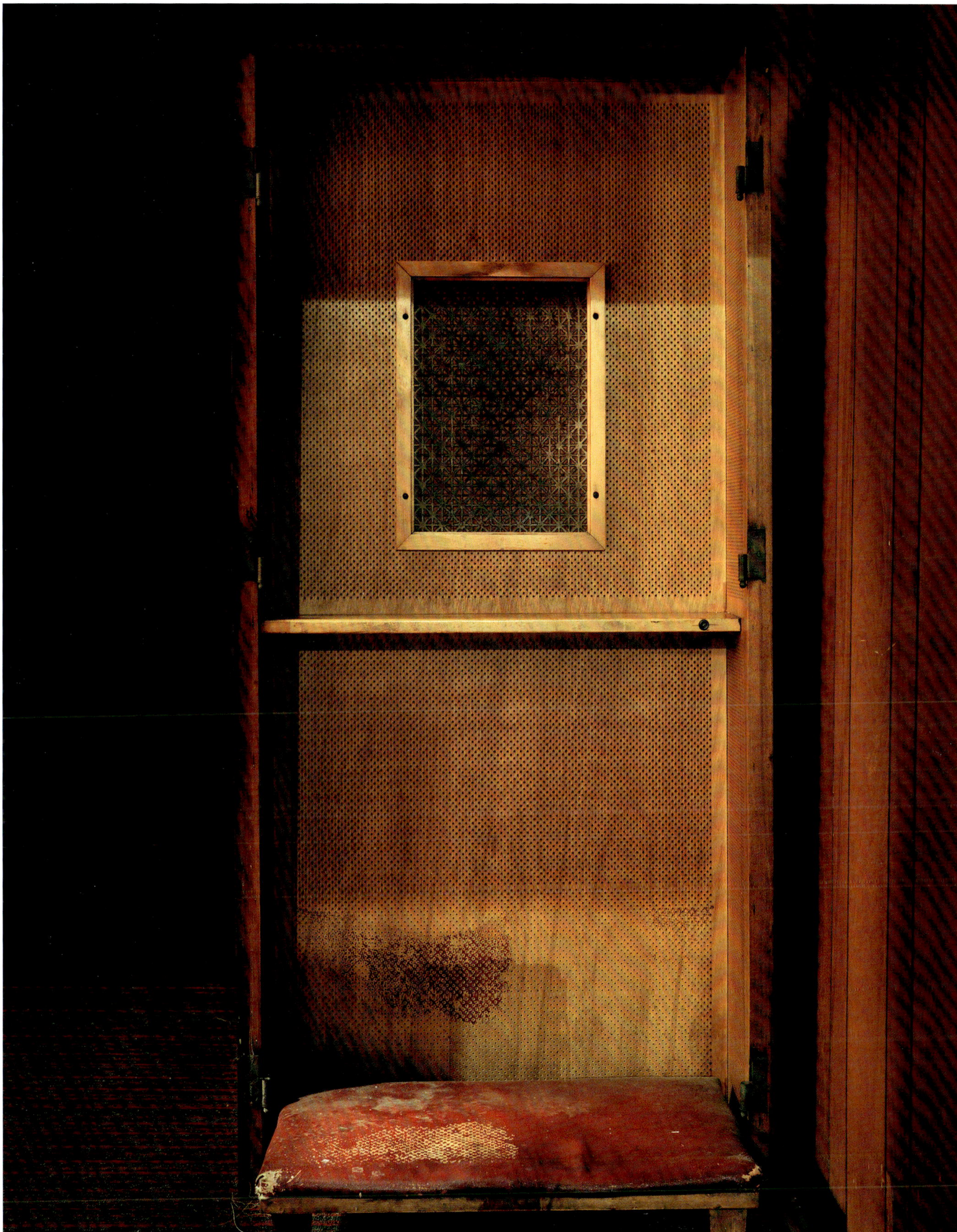

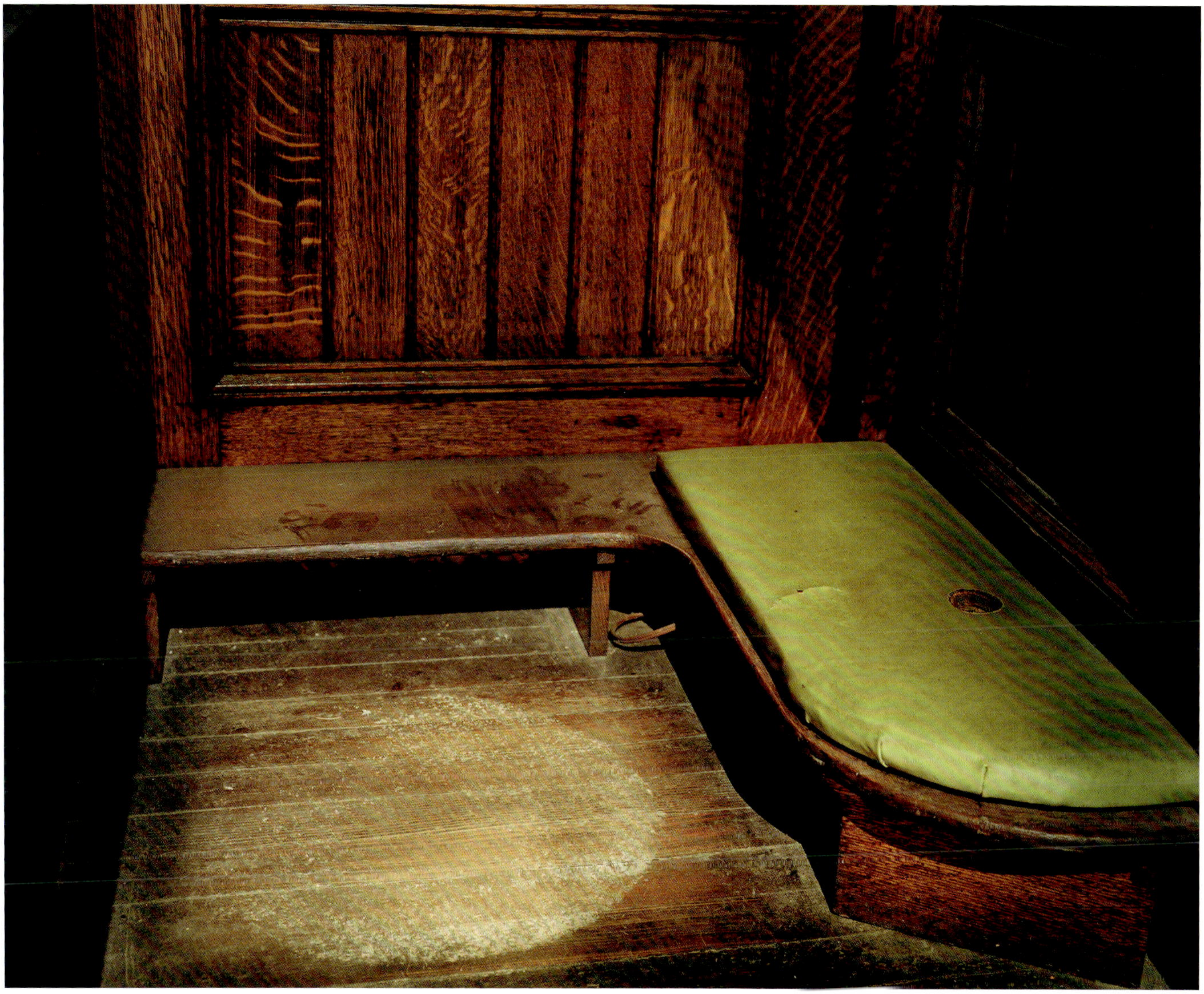

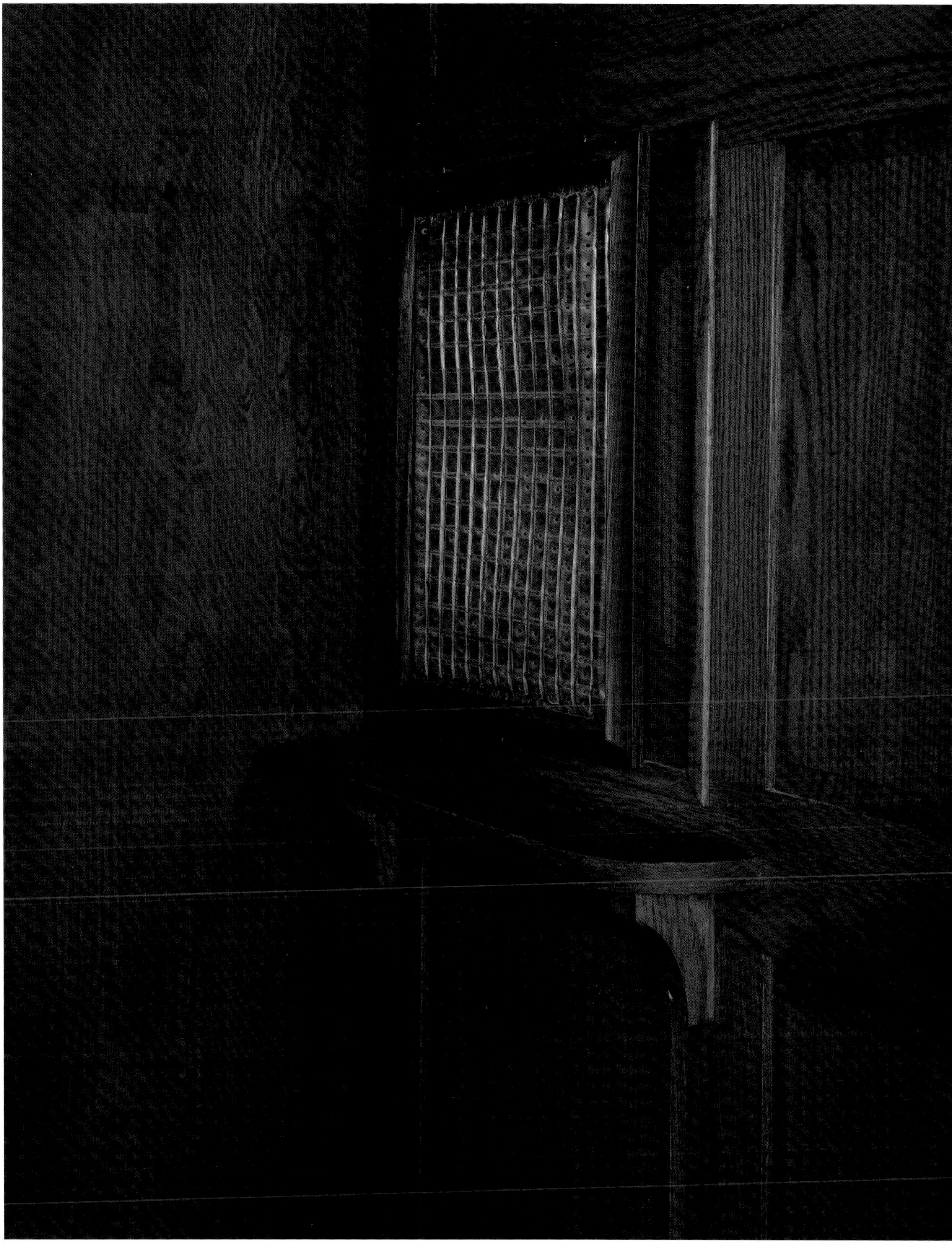

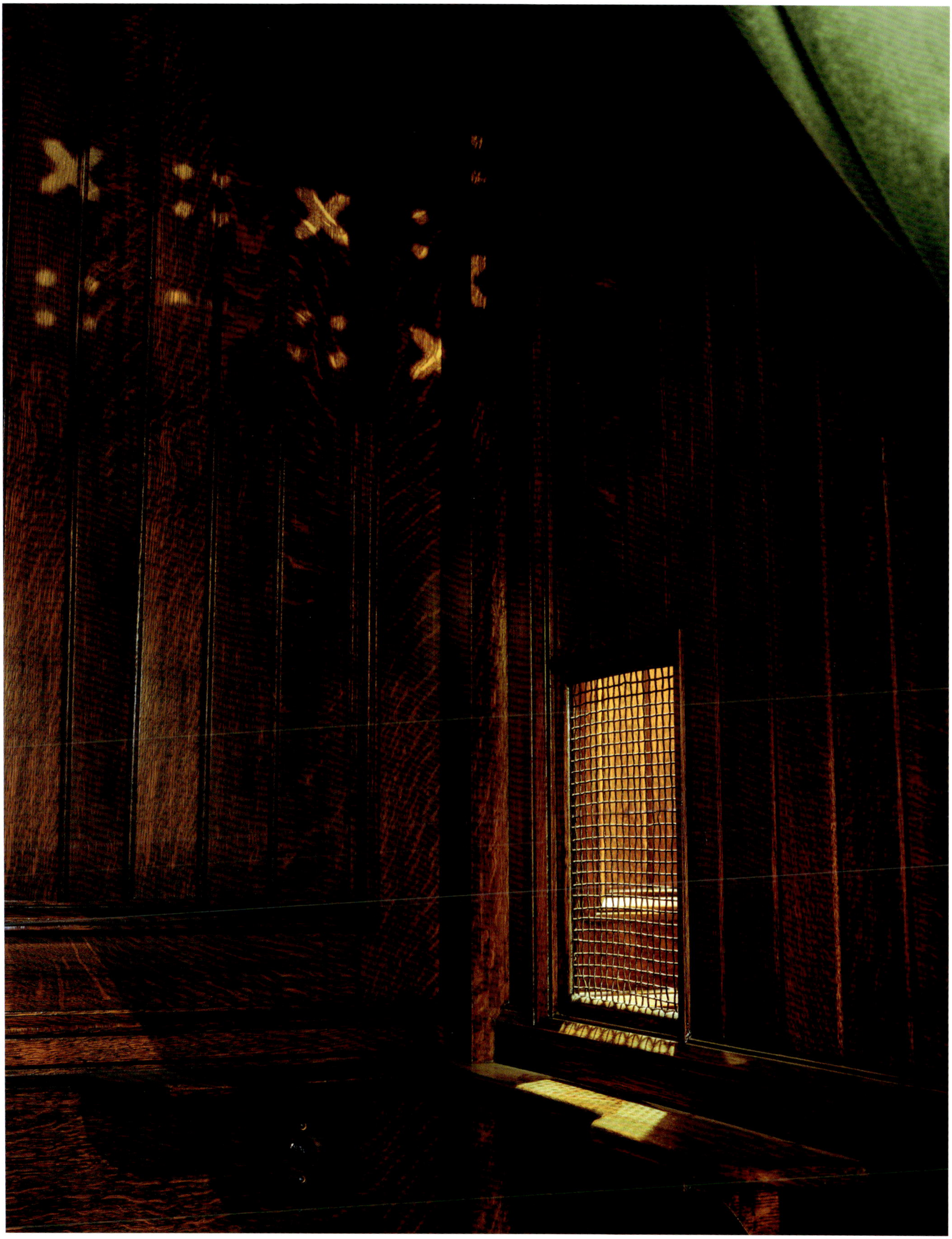

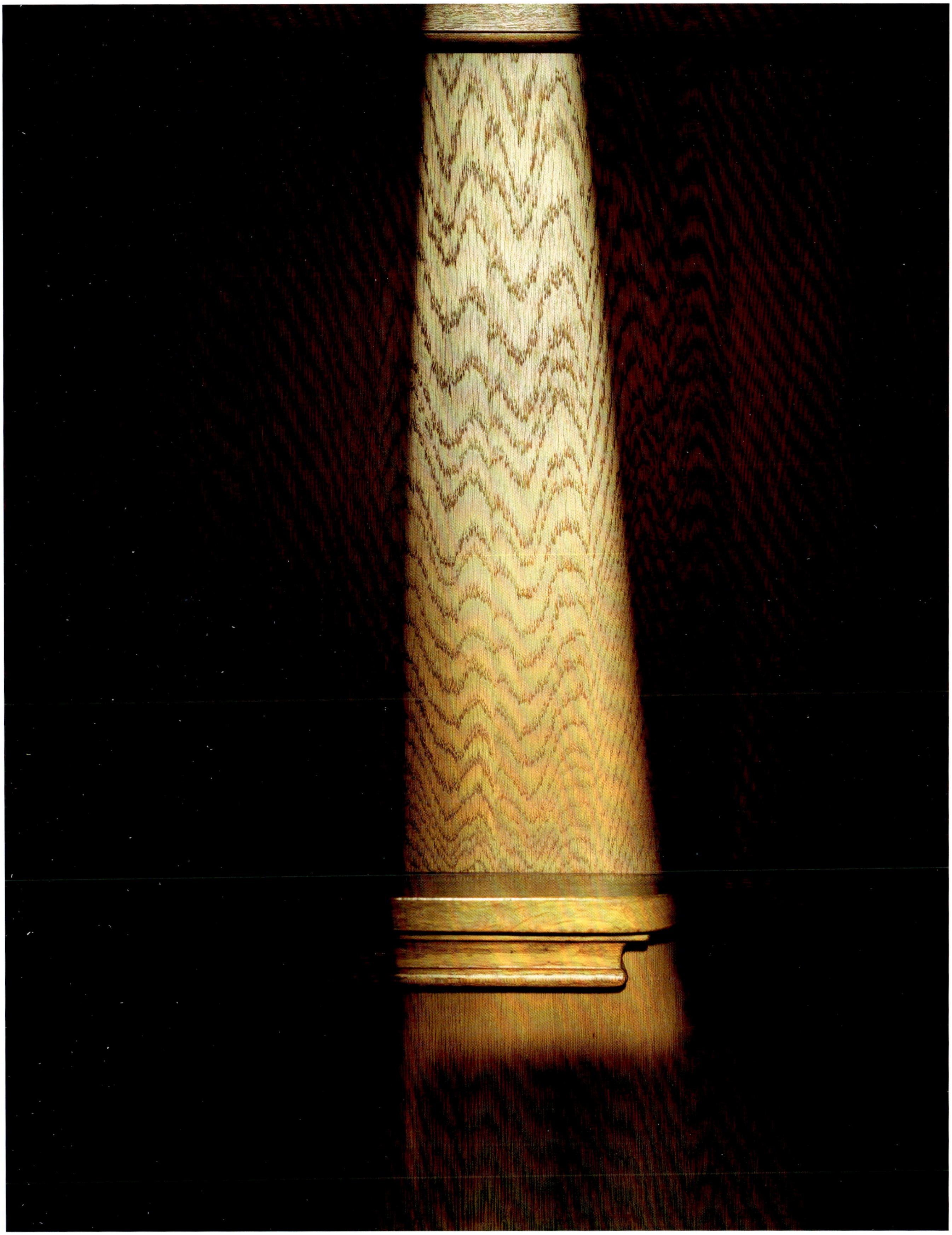

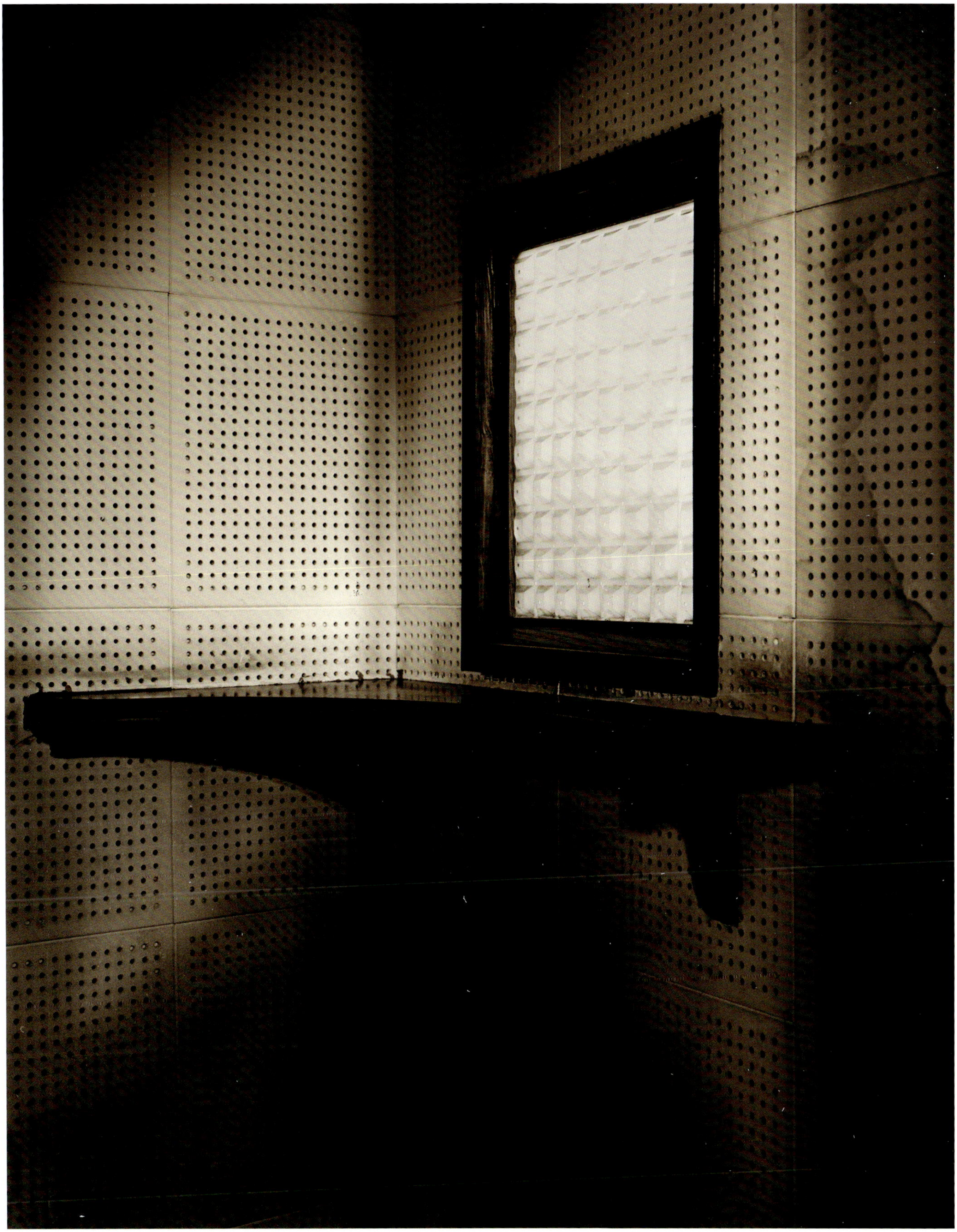

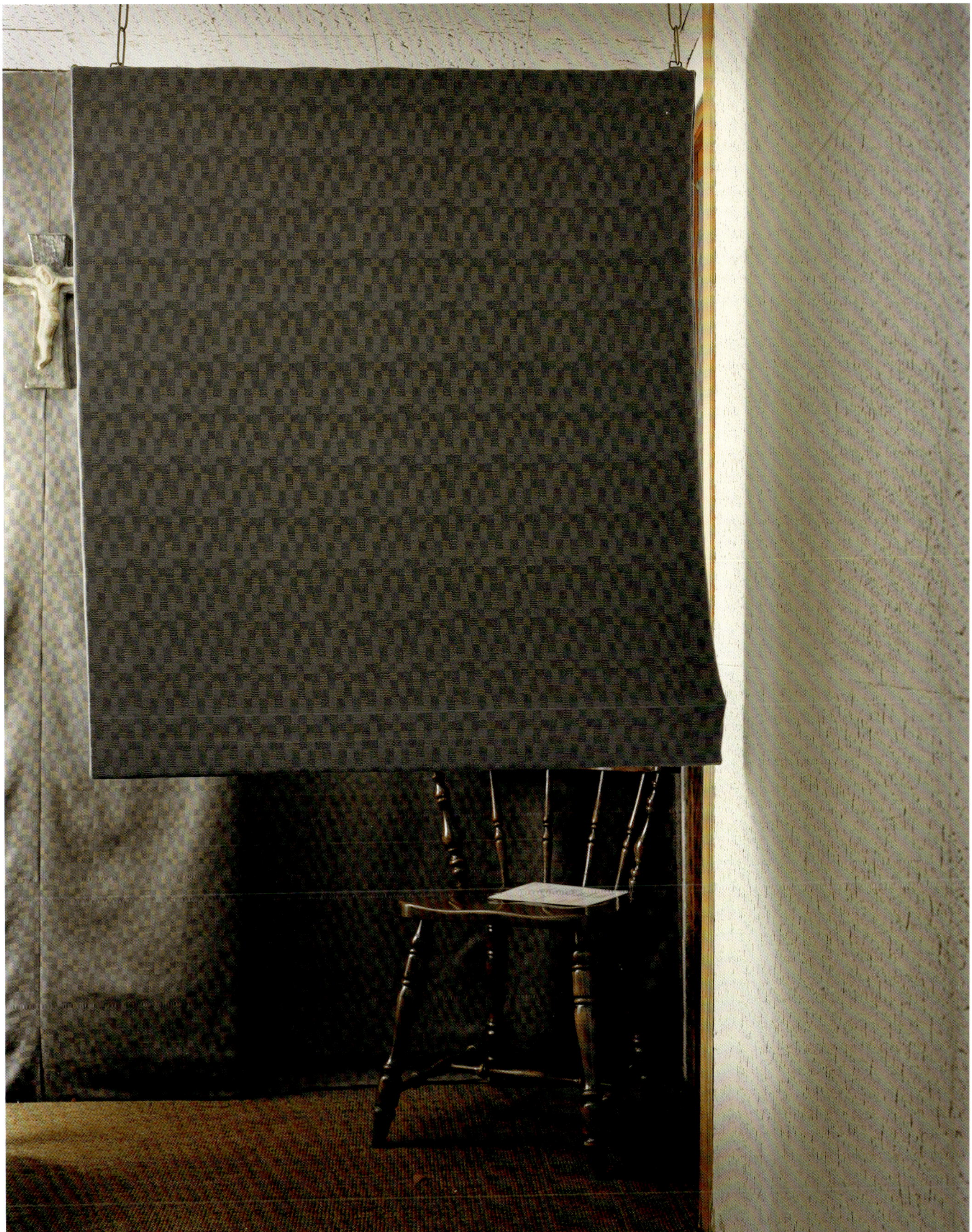

2.

Saint Francis of Assisi
Saint Anthony of Padua
Saint Paul the Apostle
Saint Malachy
Our Lady of Częstochowa
Holy Trinity
Our Lady of Pompeii
Saint Valentine

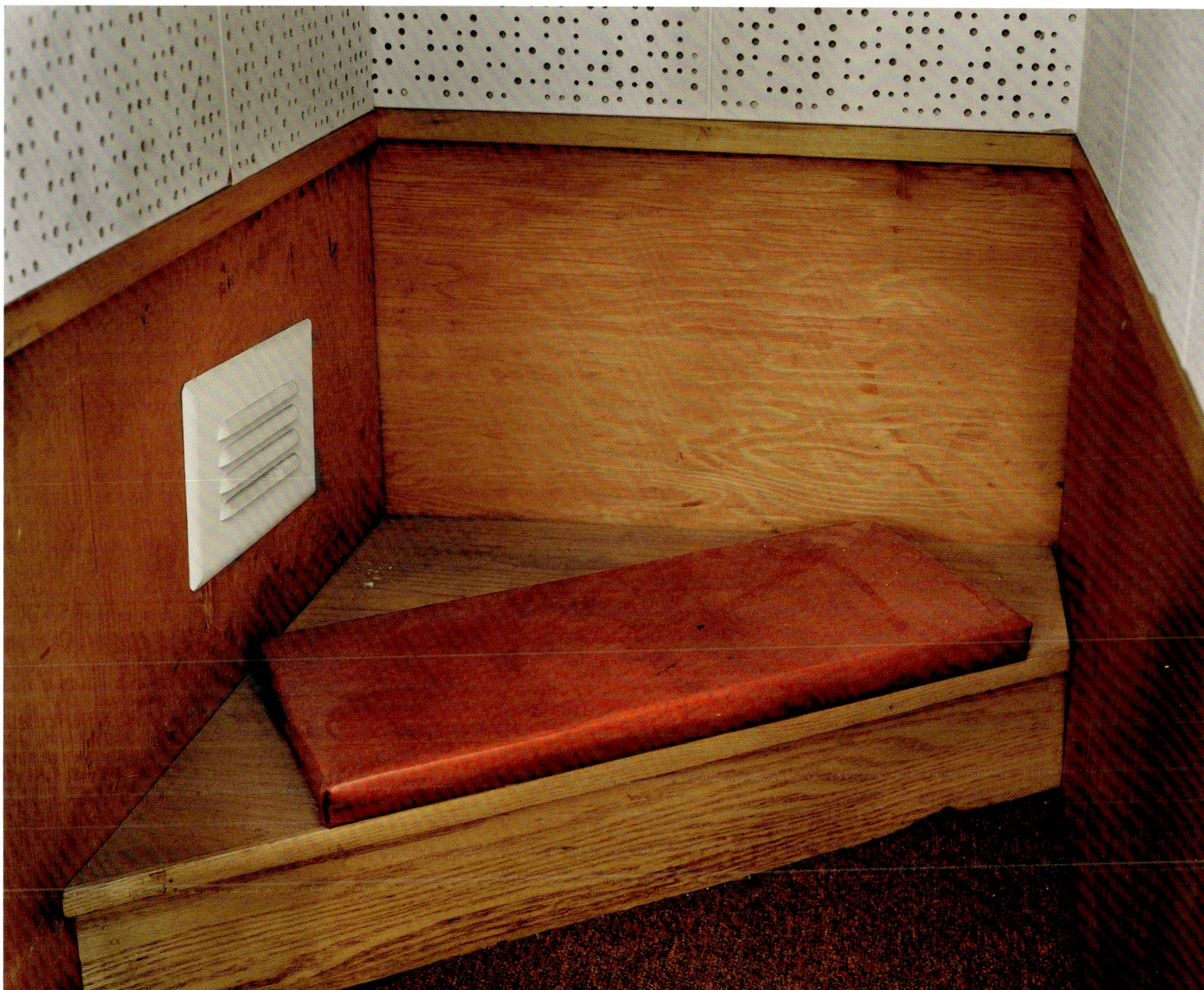

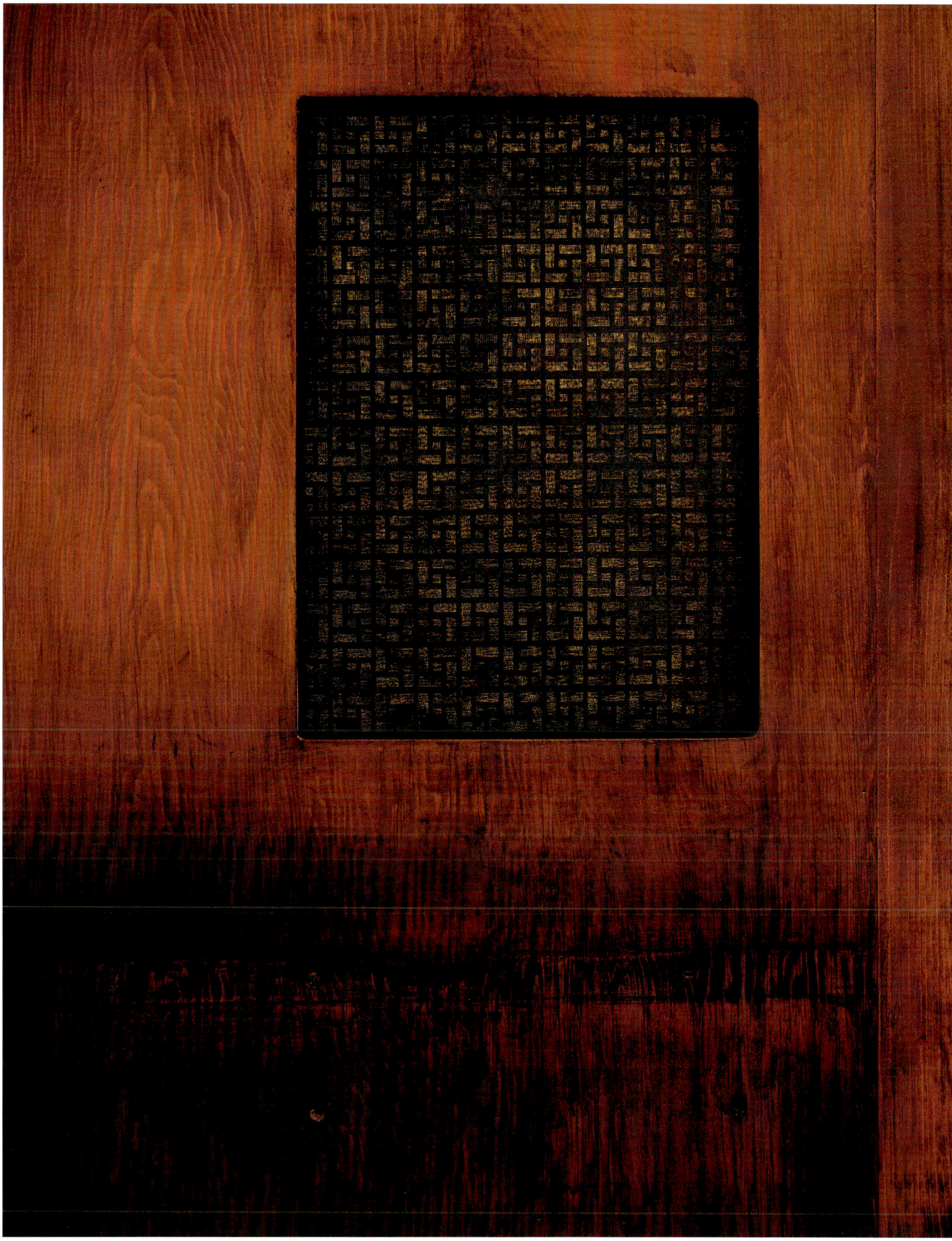

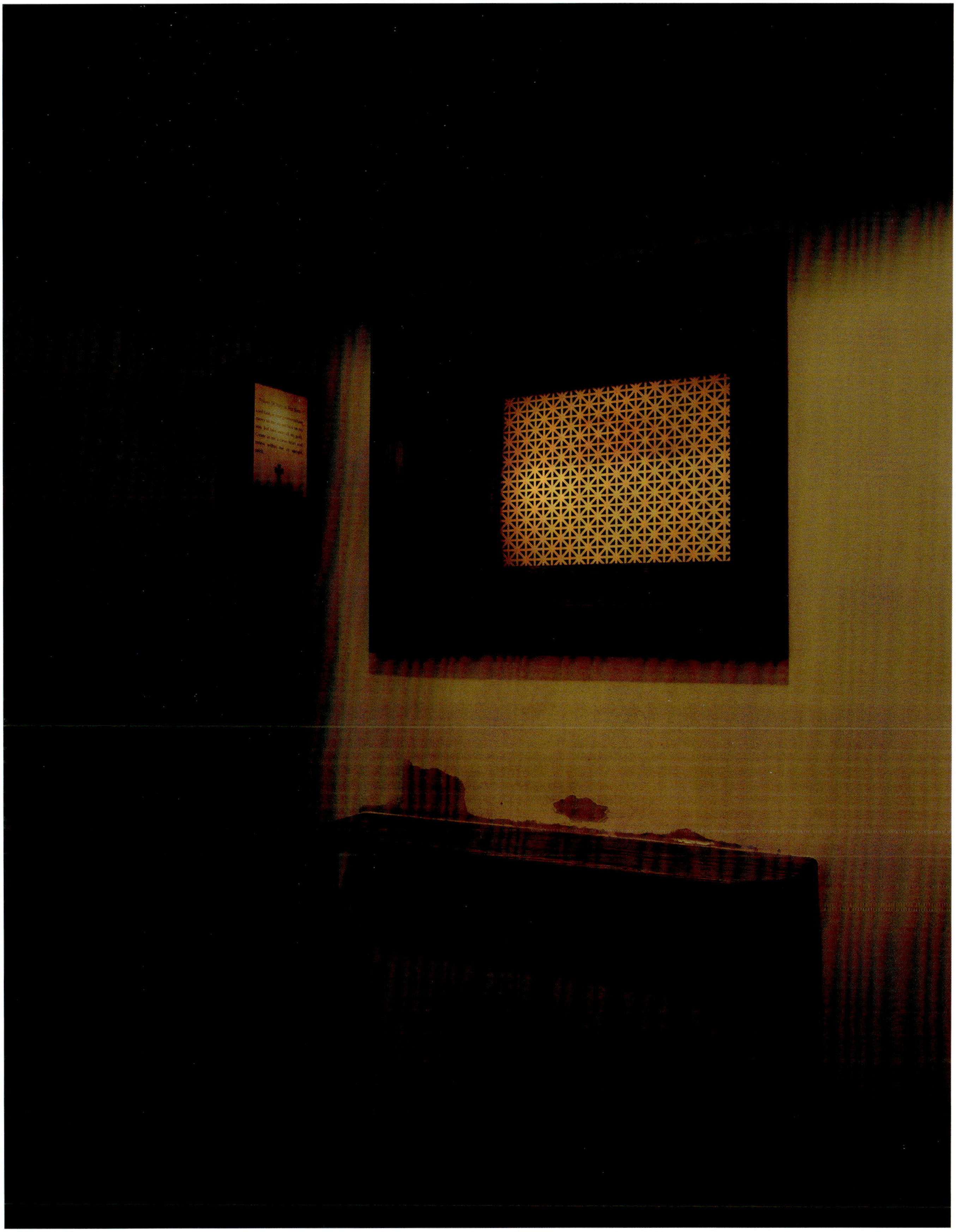

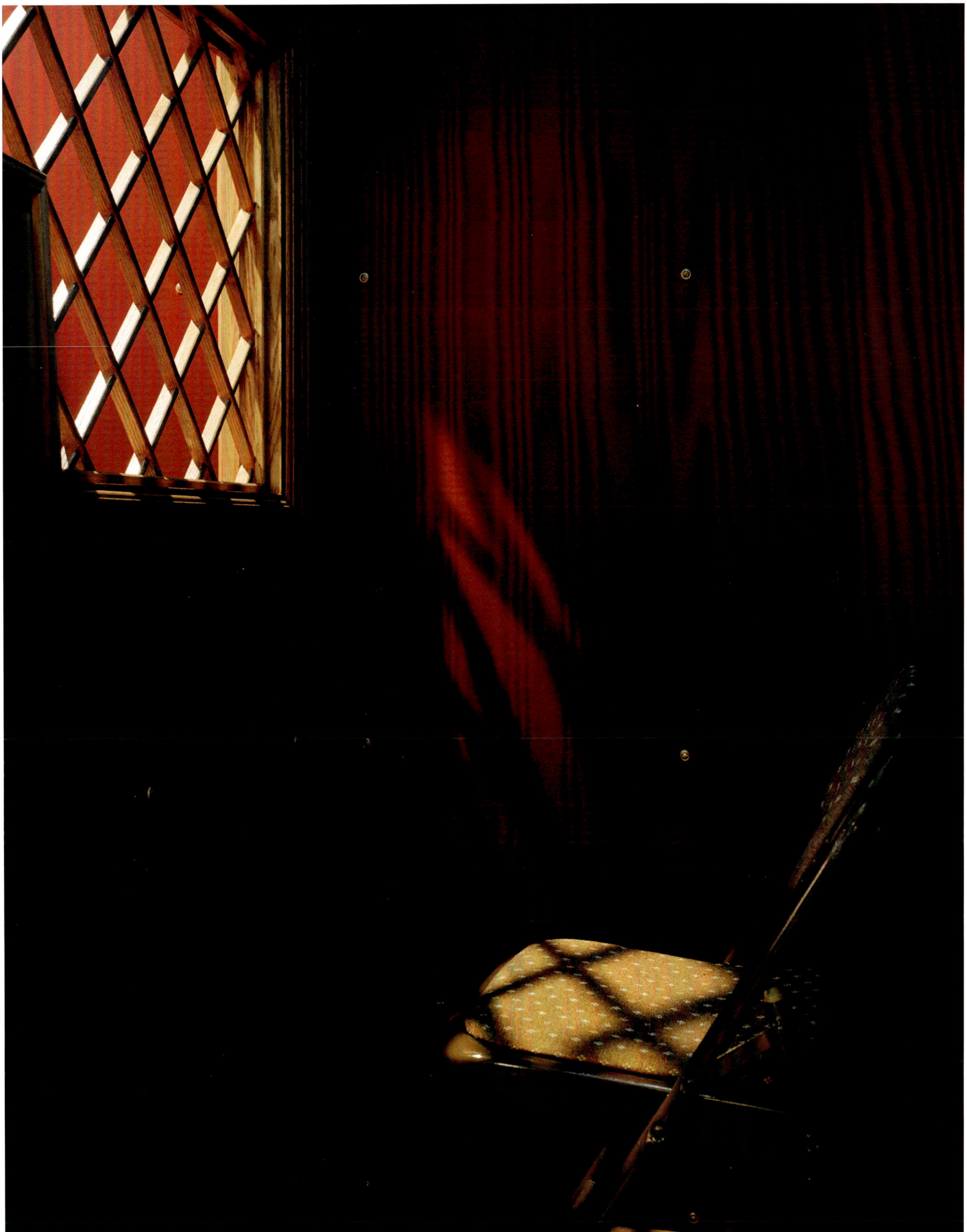

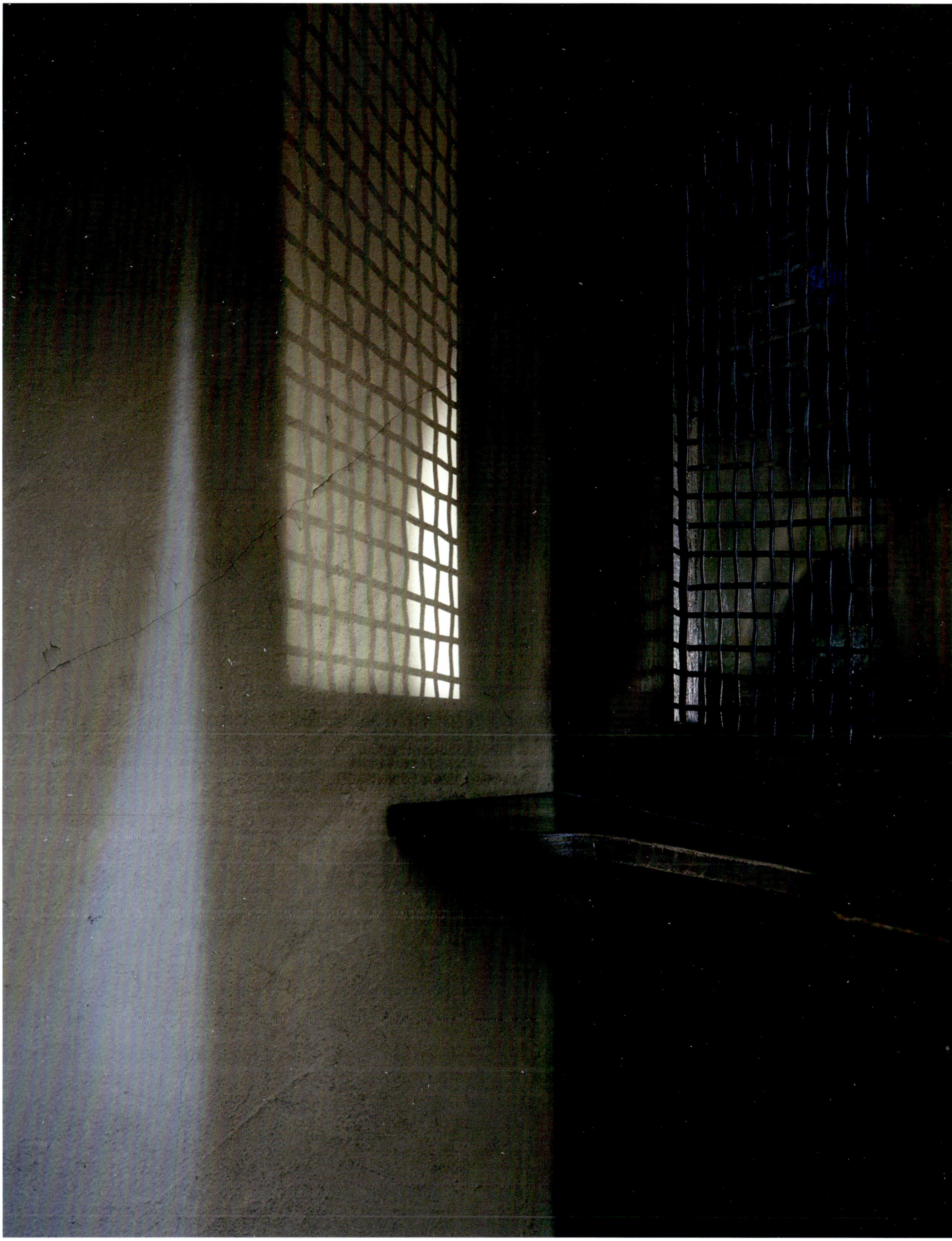

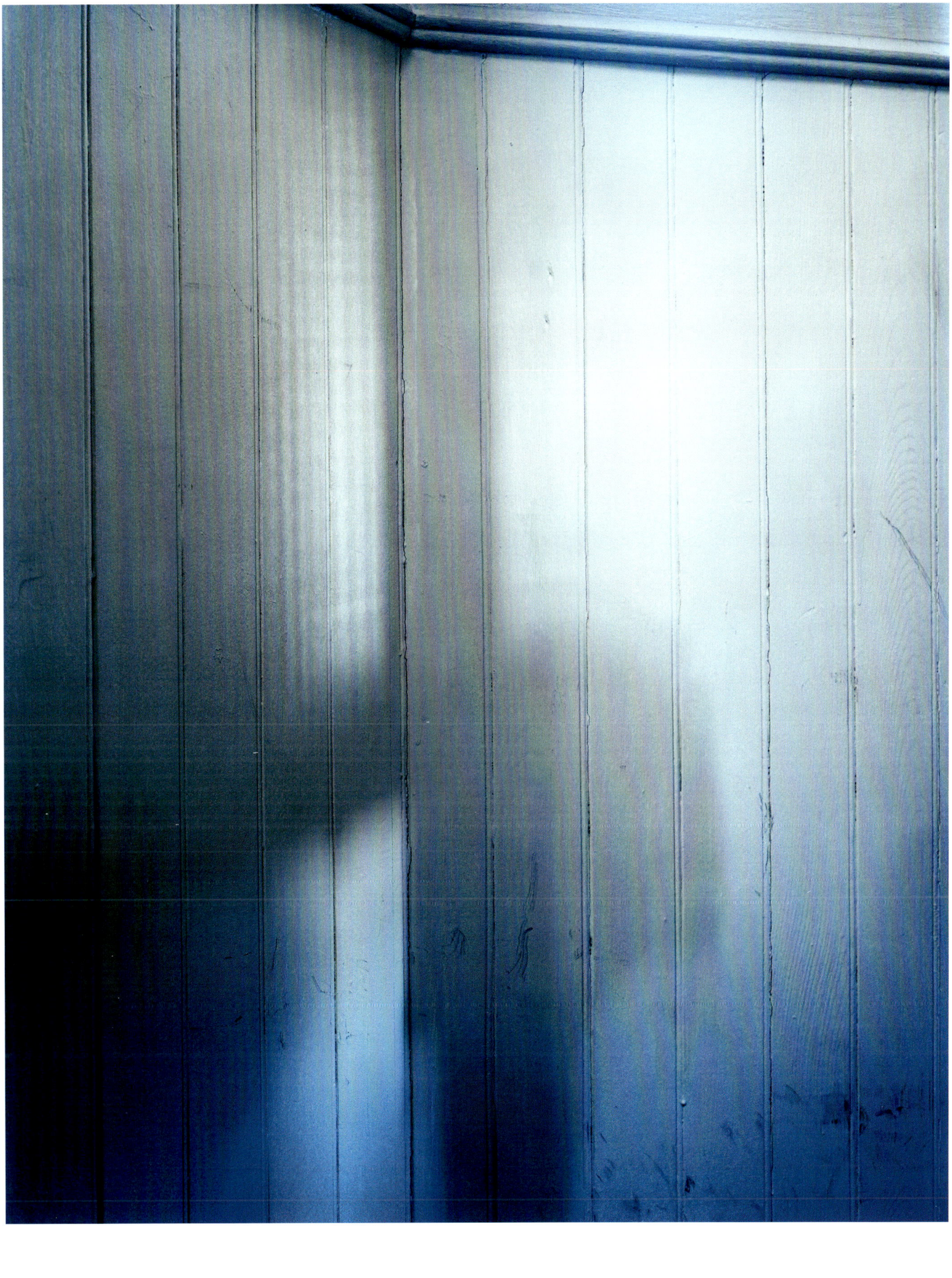

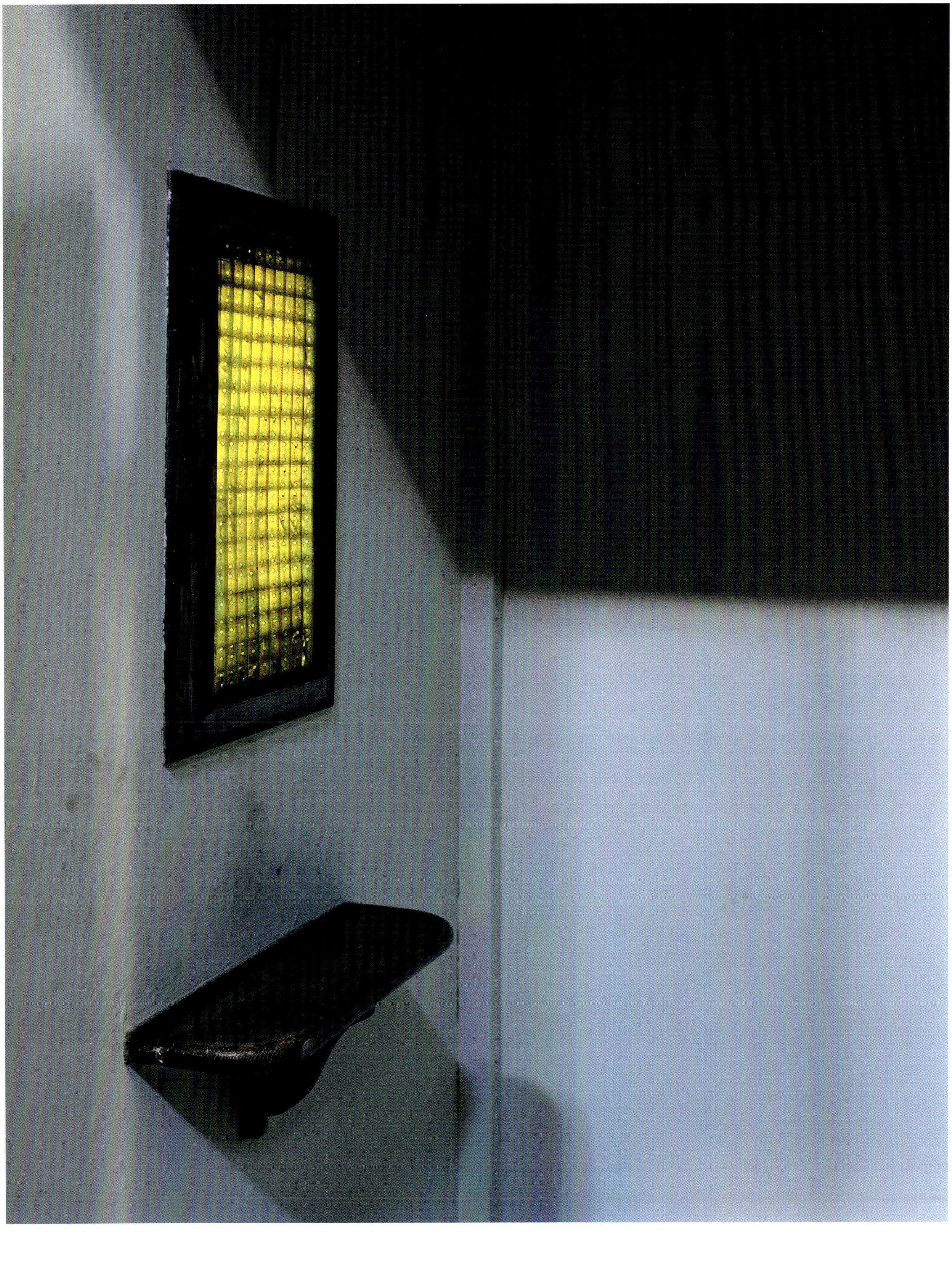

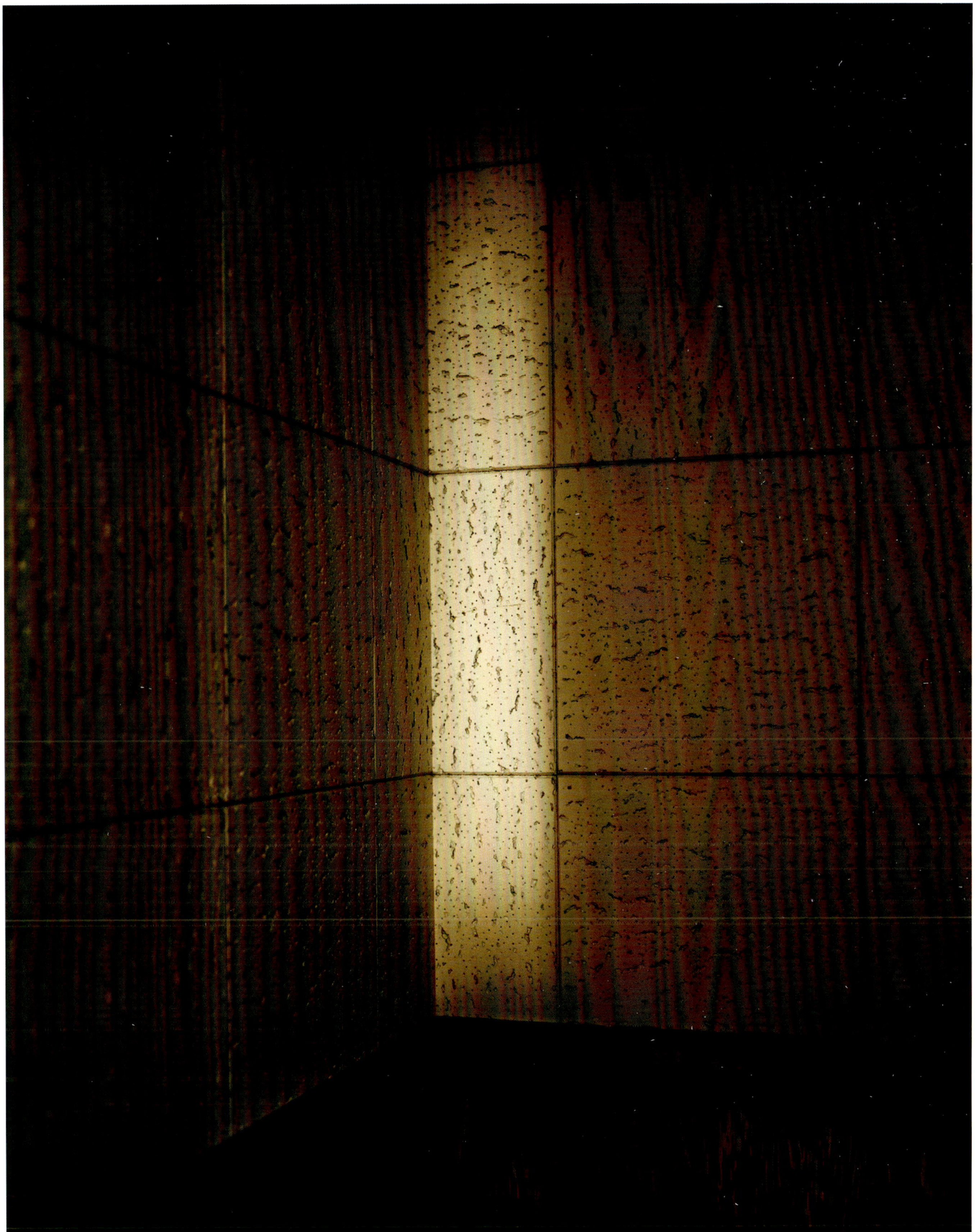

3.
Our Lady of Victory
Saint Rose of Lima
Holy Family
Saint Joseph
Saint Pancras
Our Lady of Good Counsel
Notre Dame
Ascension

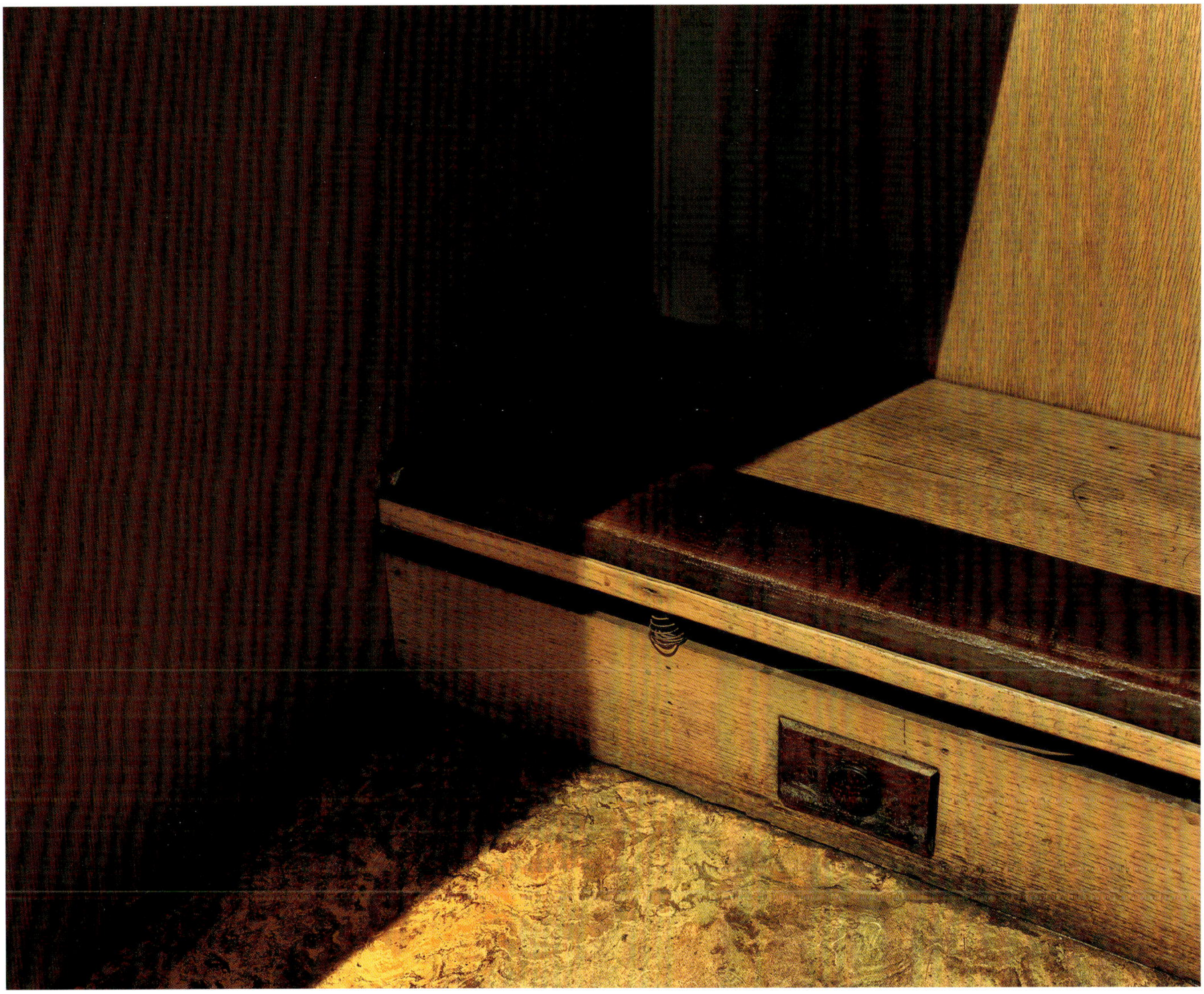

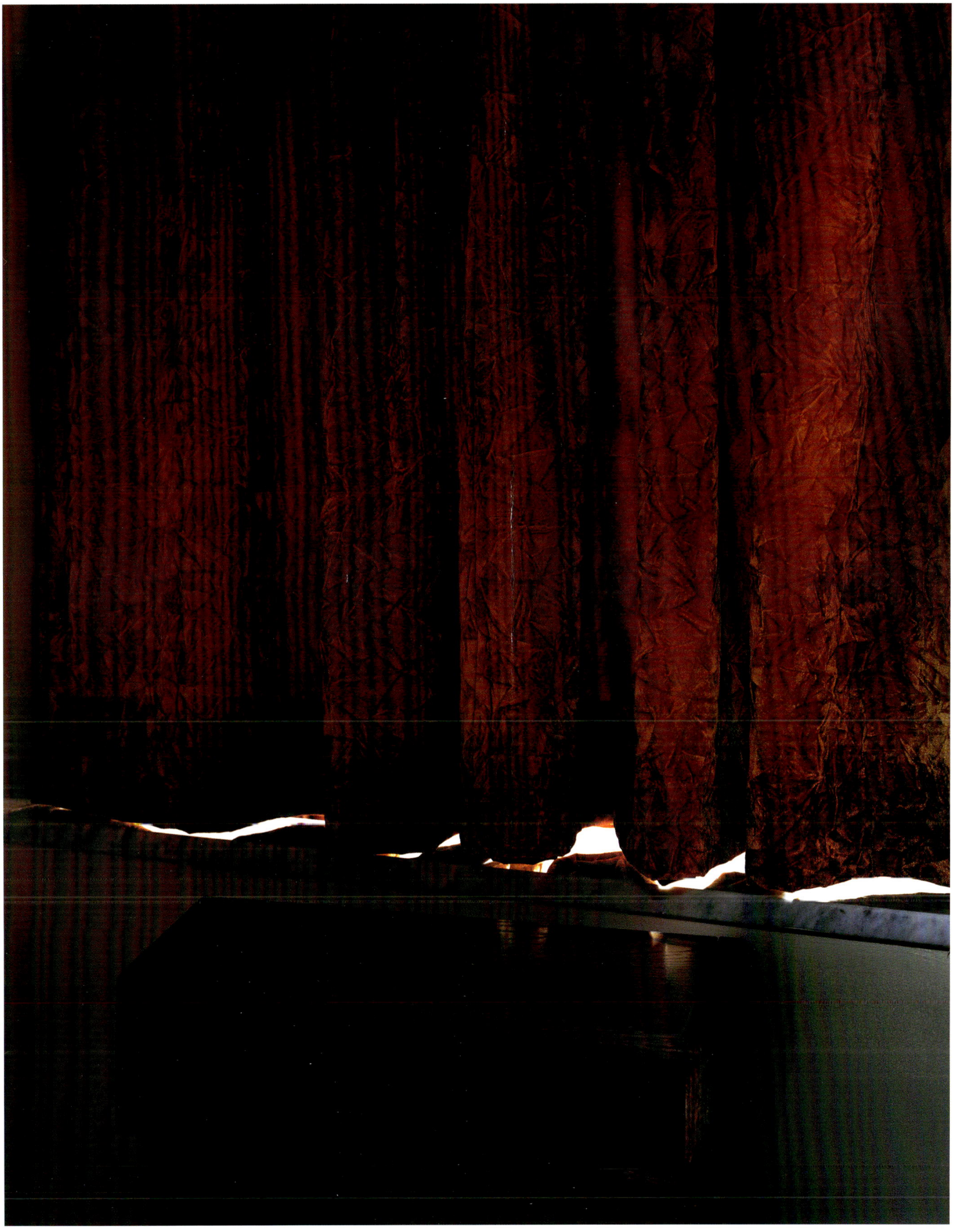

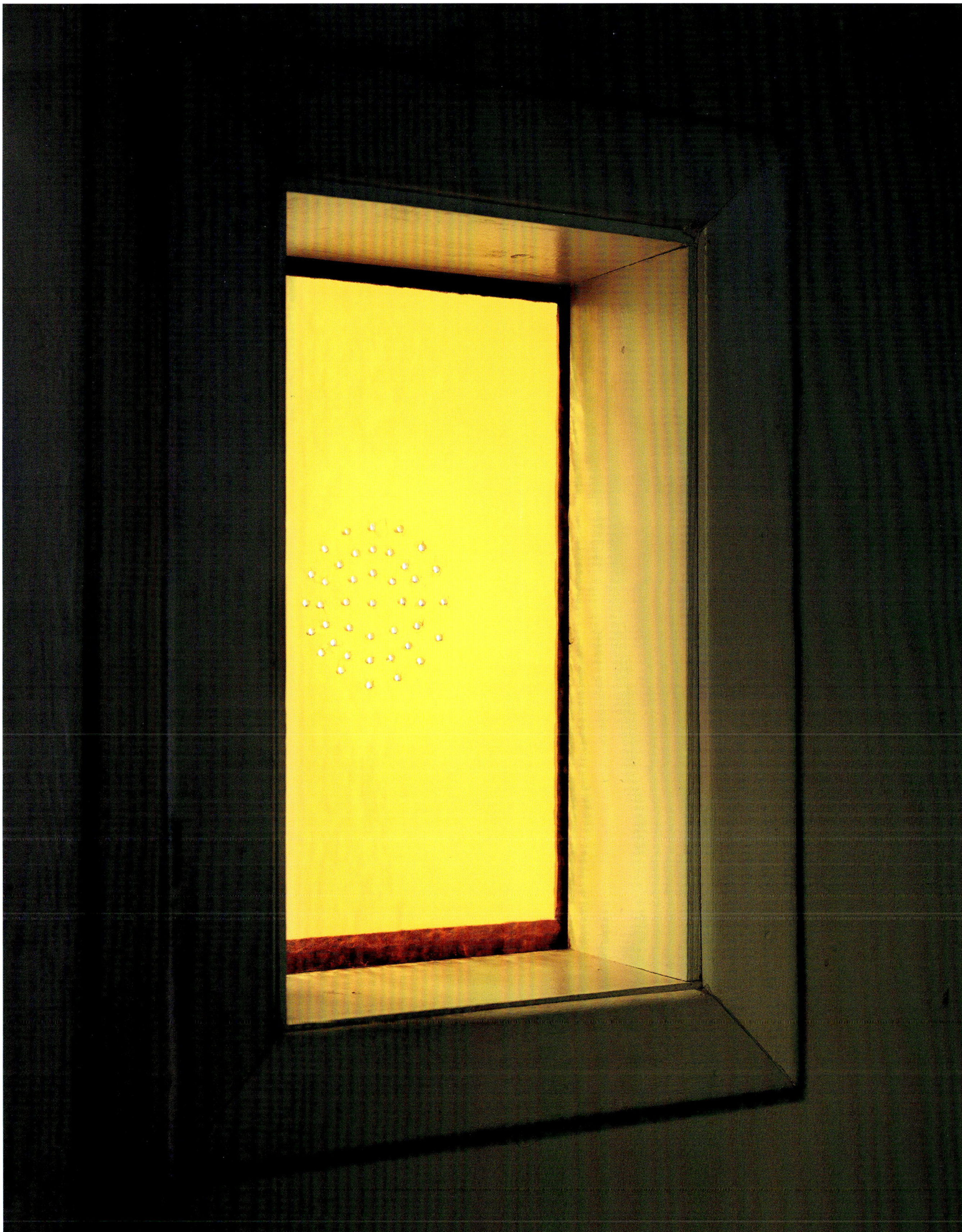

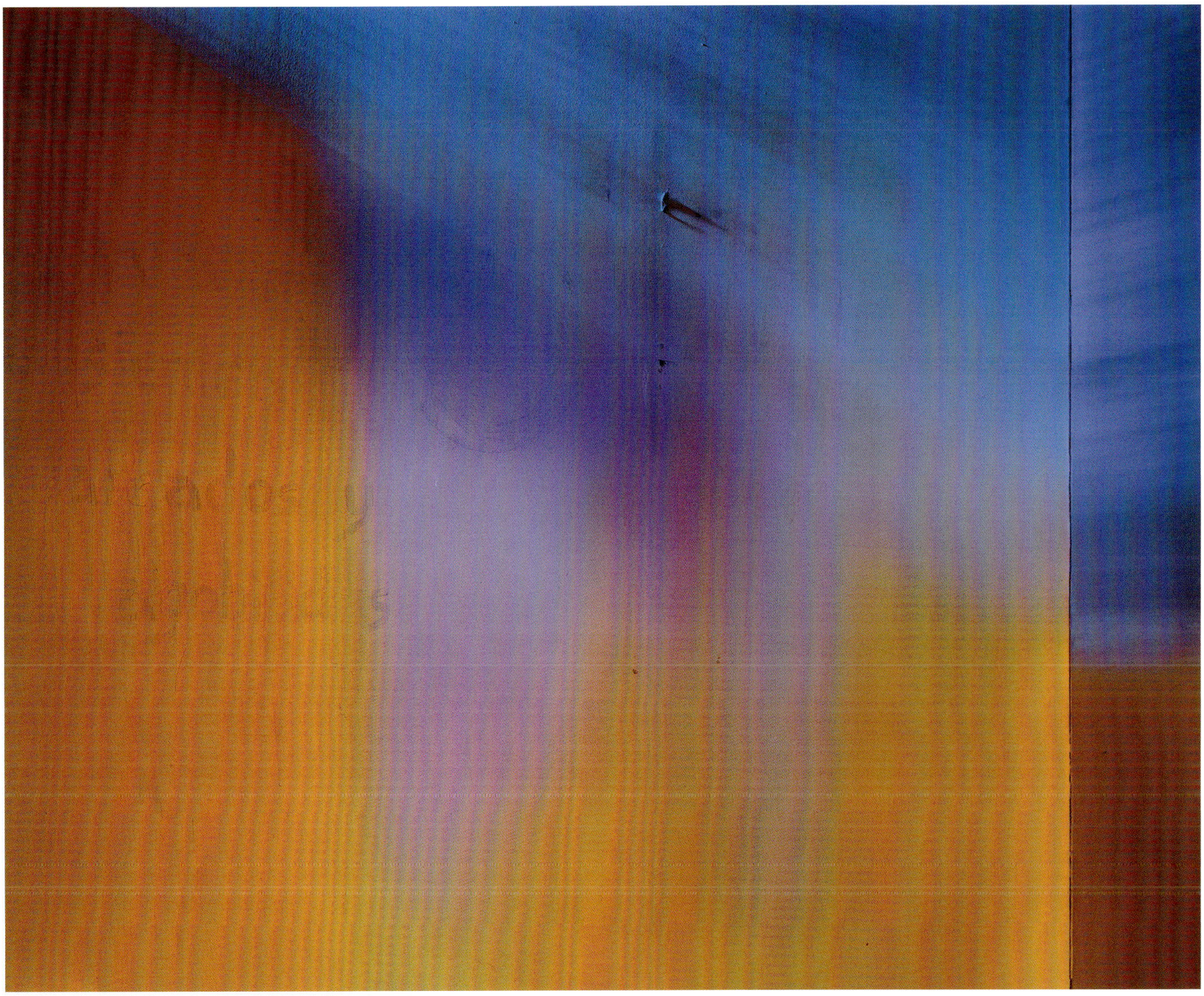

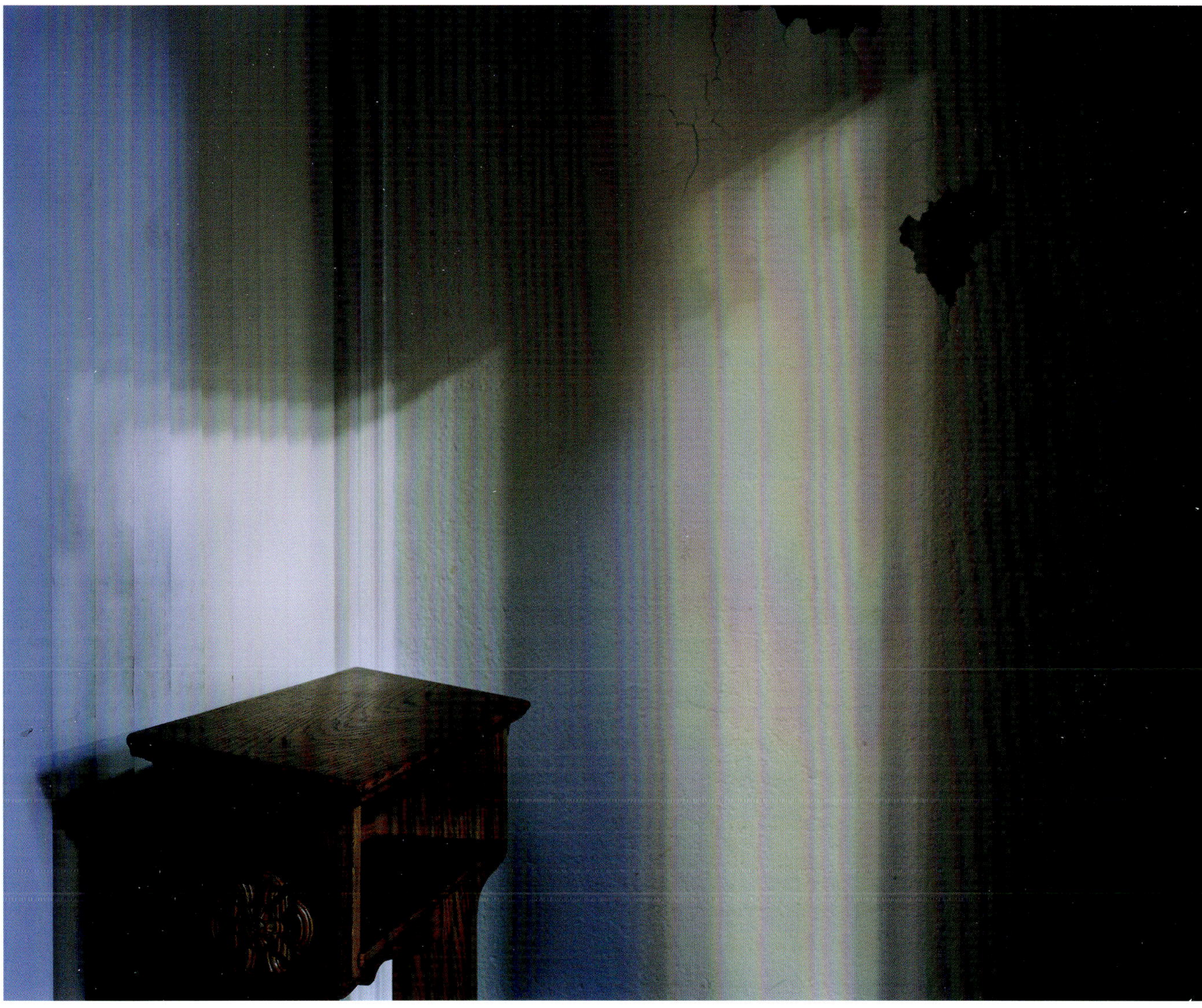

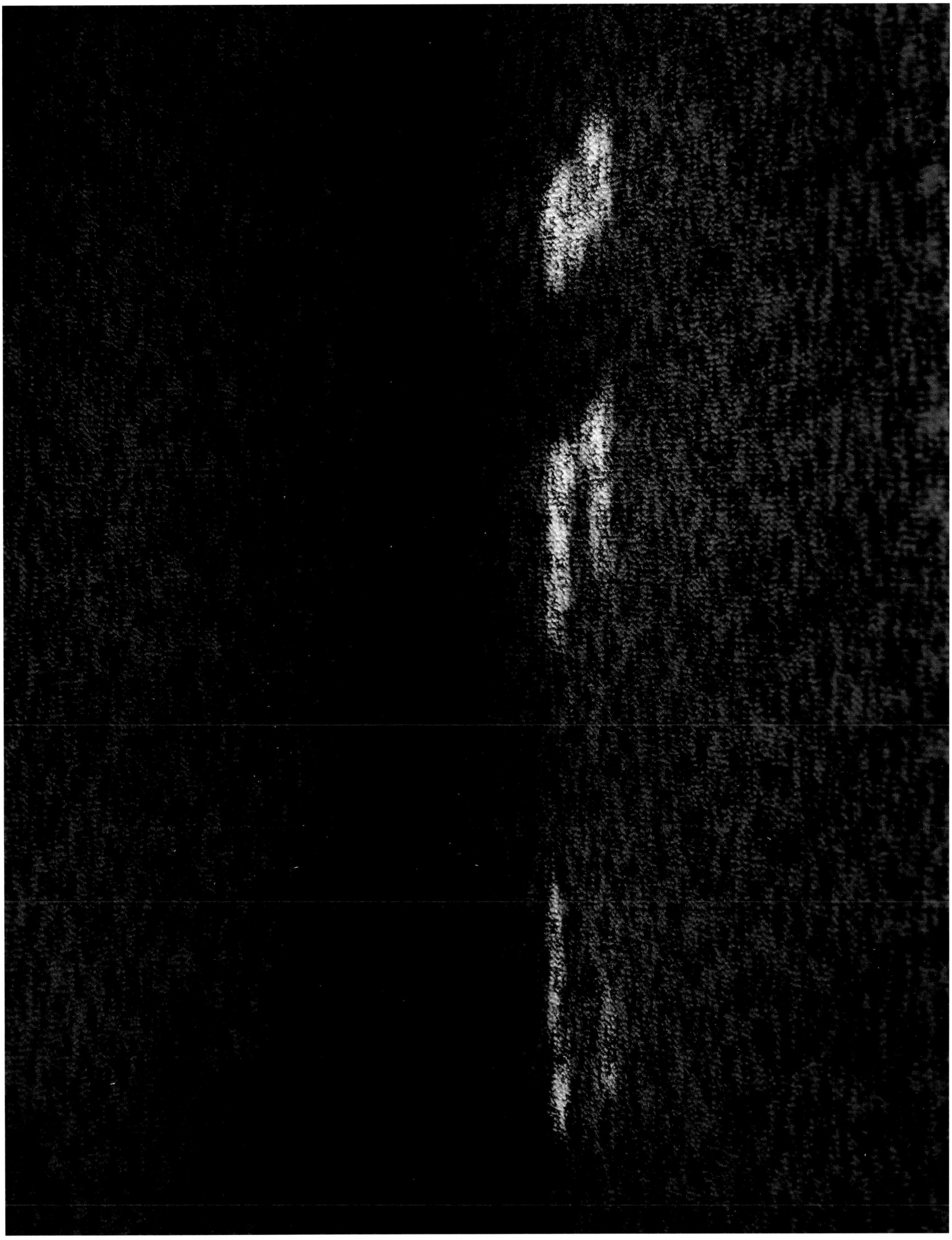

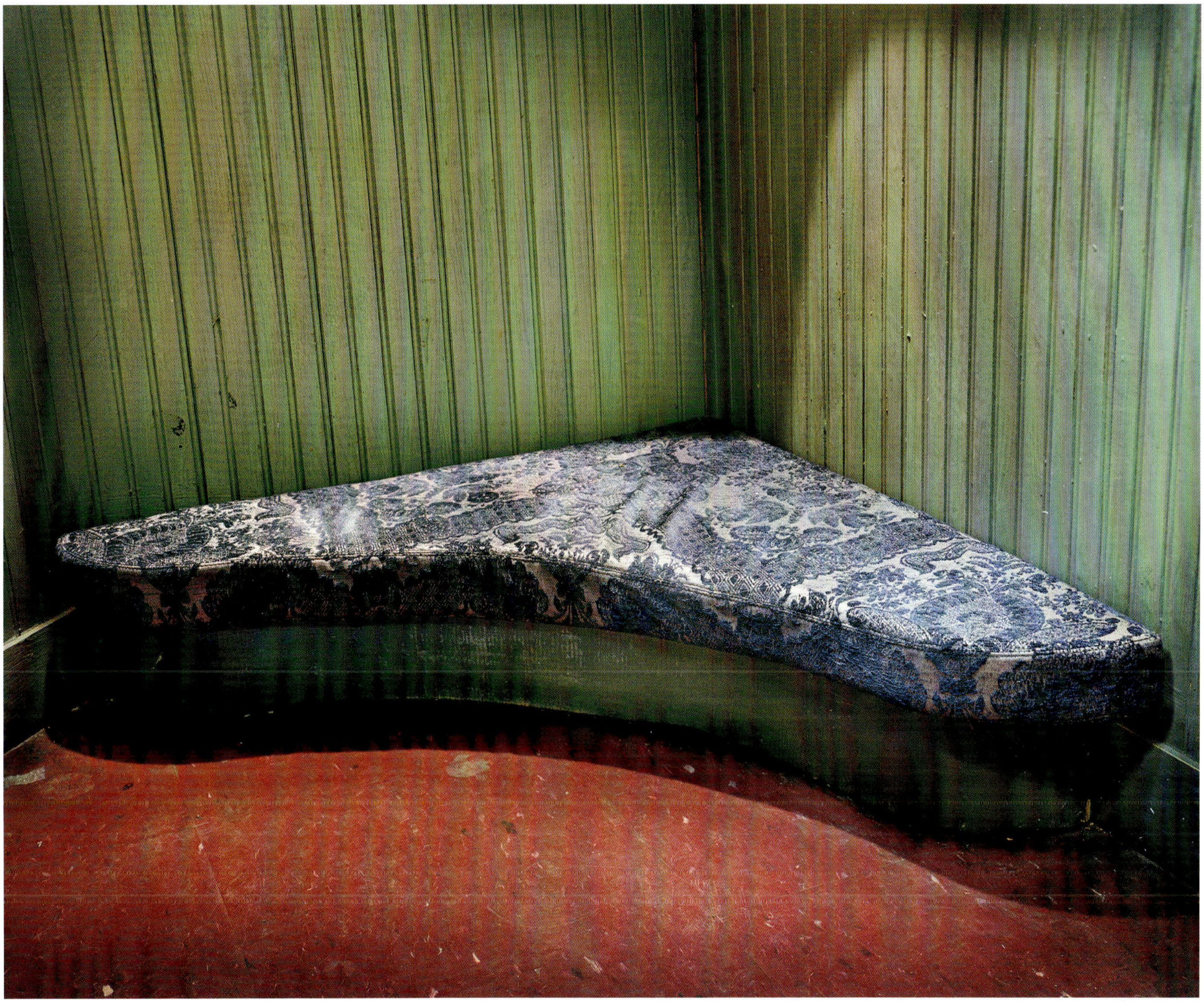

4.

Most Holy Redeemer
Our Lady of Perpetual Help
Saint Christopher
Saint Monica
Our Lady of Refuge
Saint Ignatius of Loyola
Saint Benedict
Saint Alphonsus

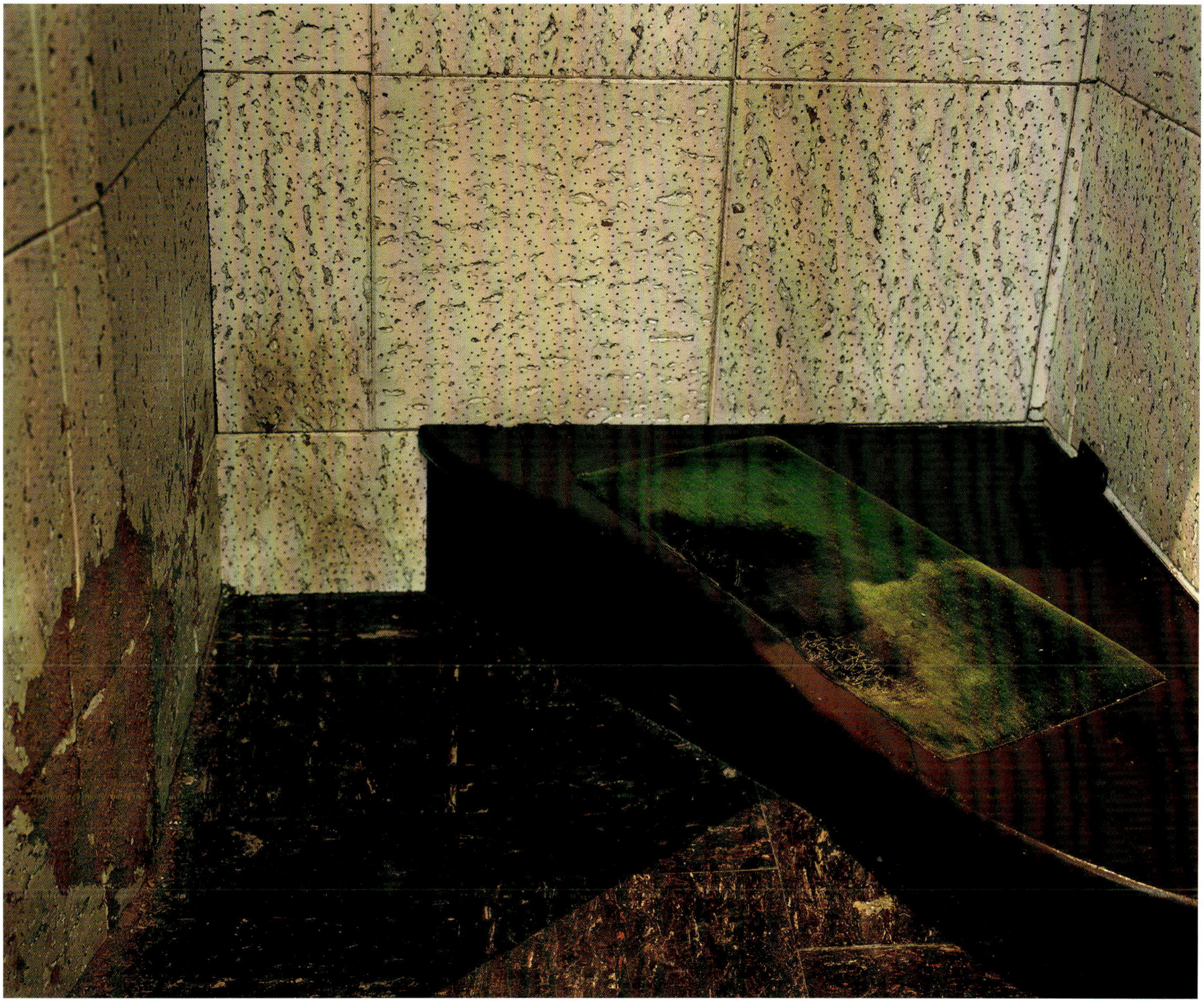

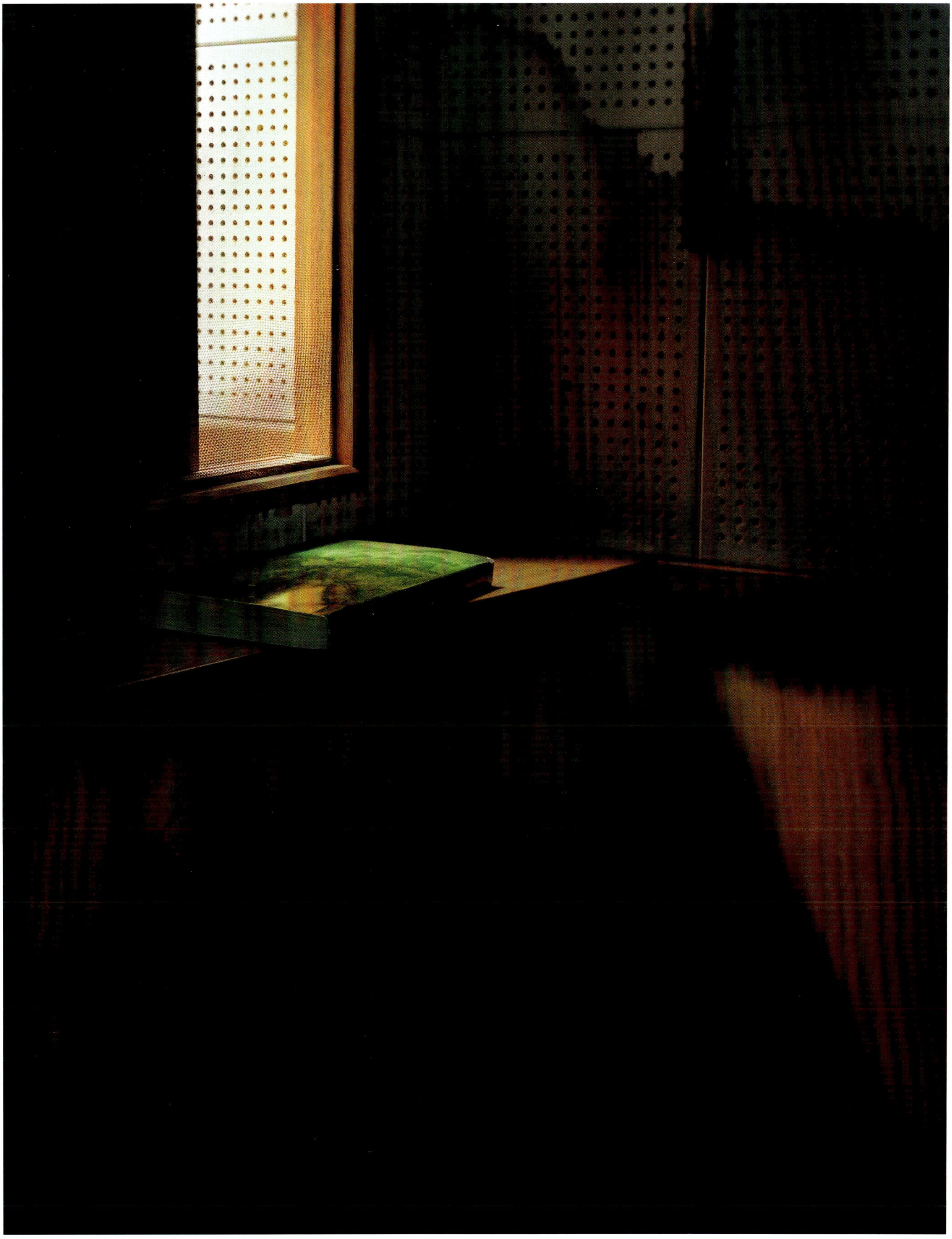

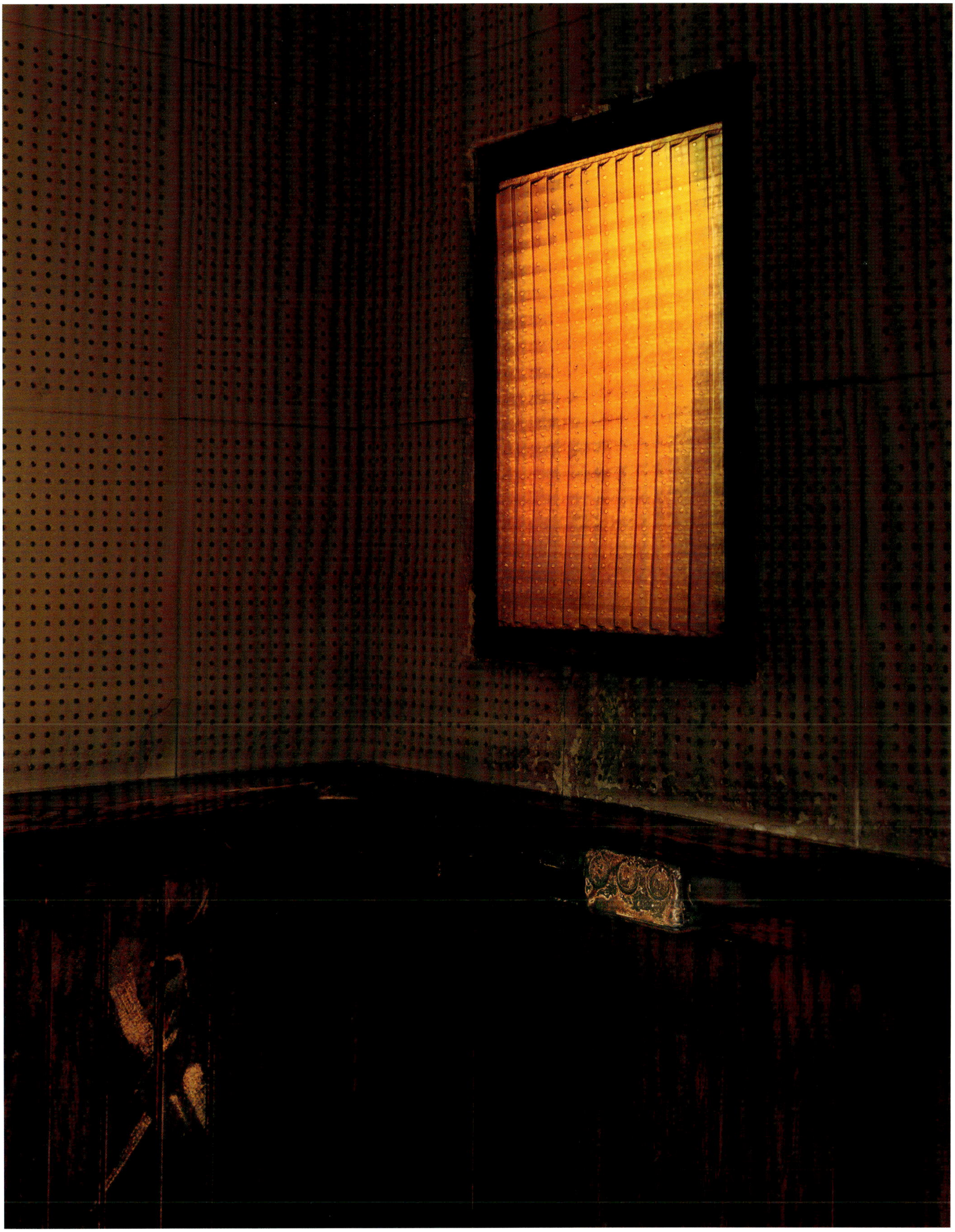

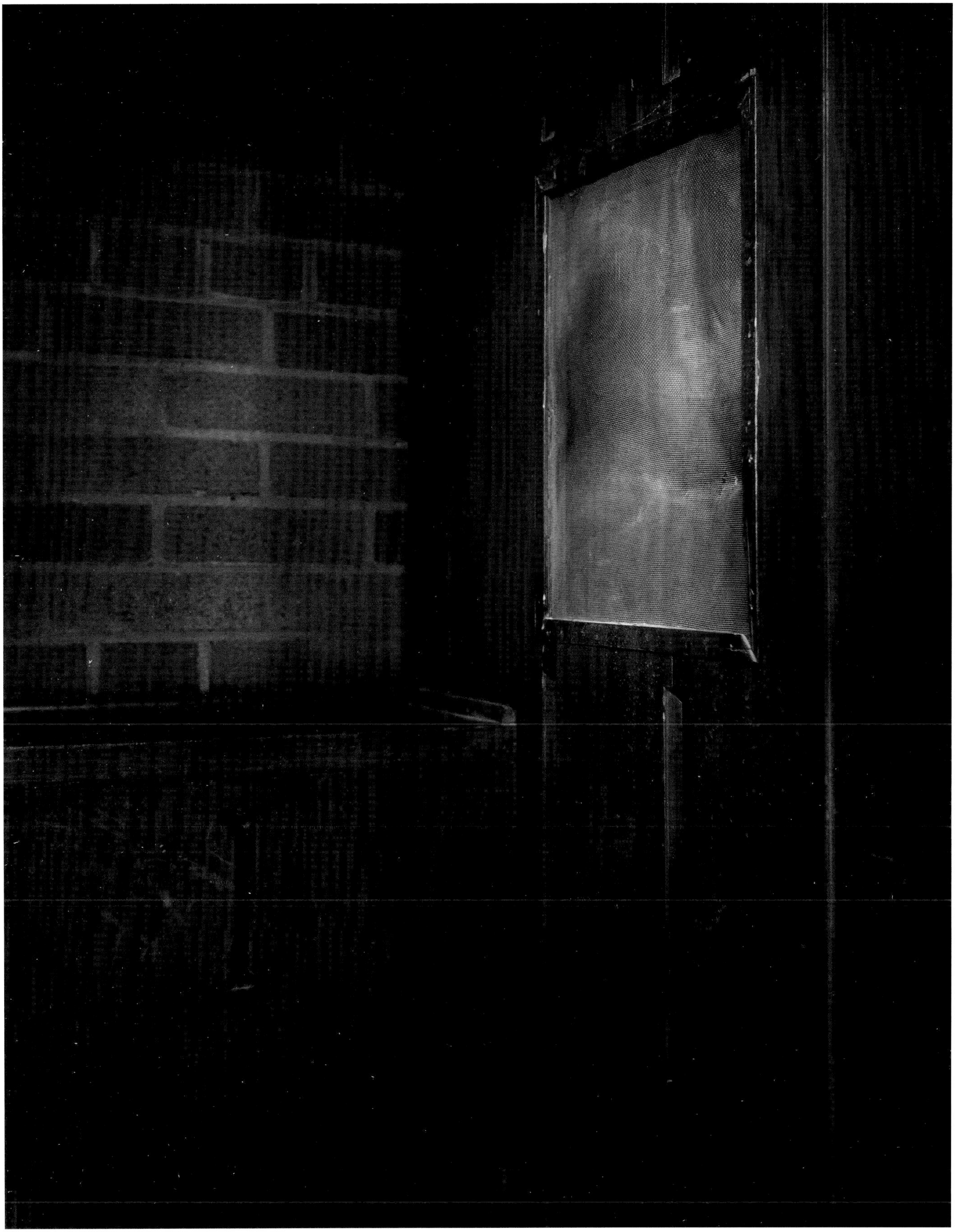

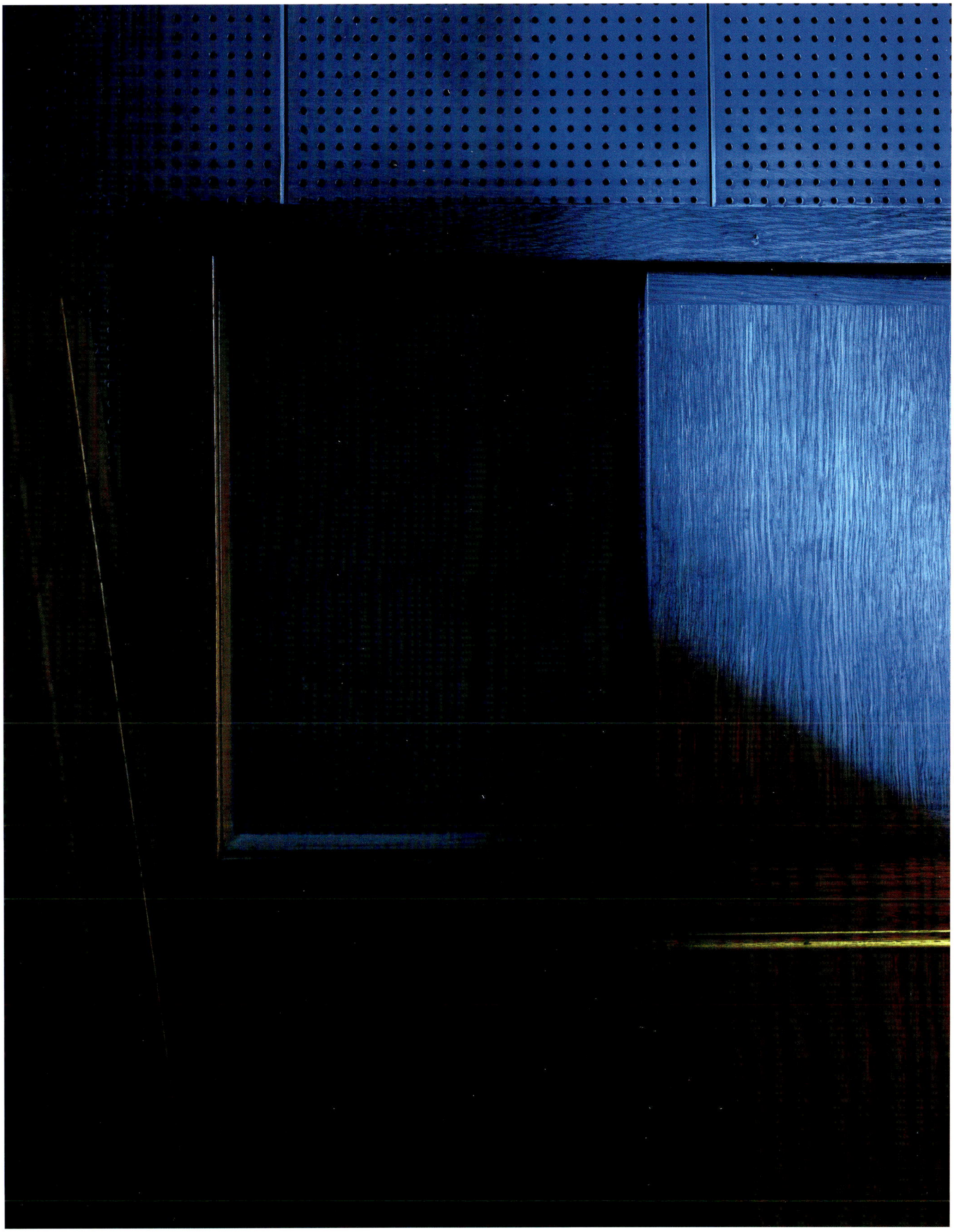

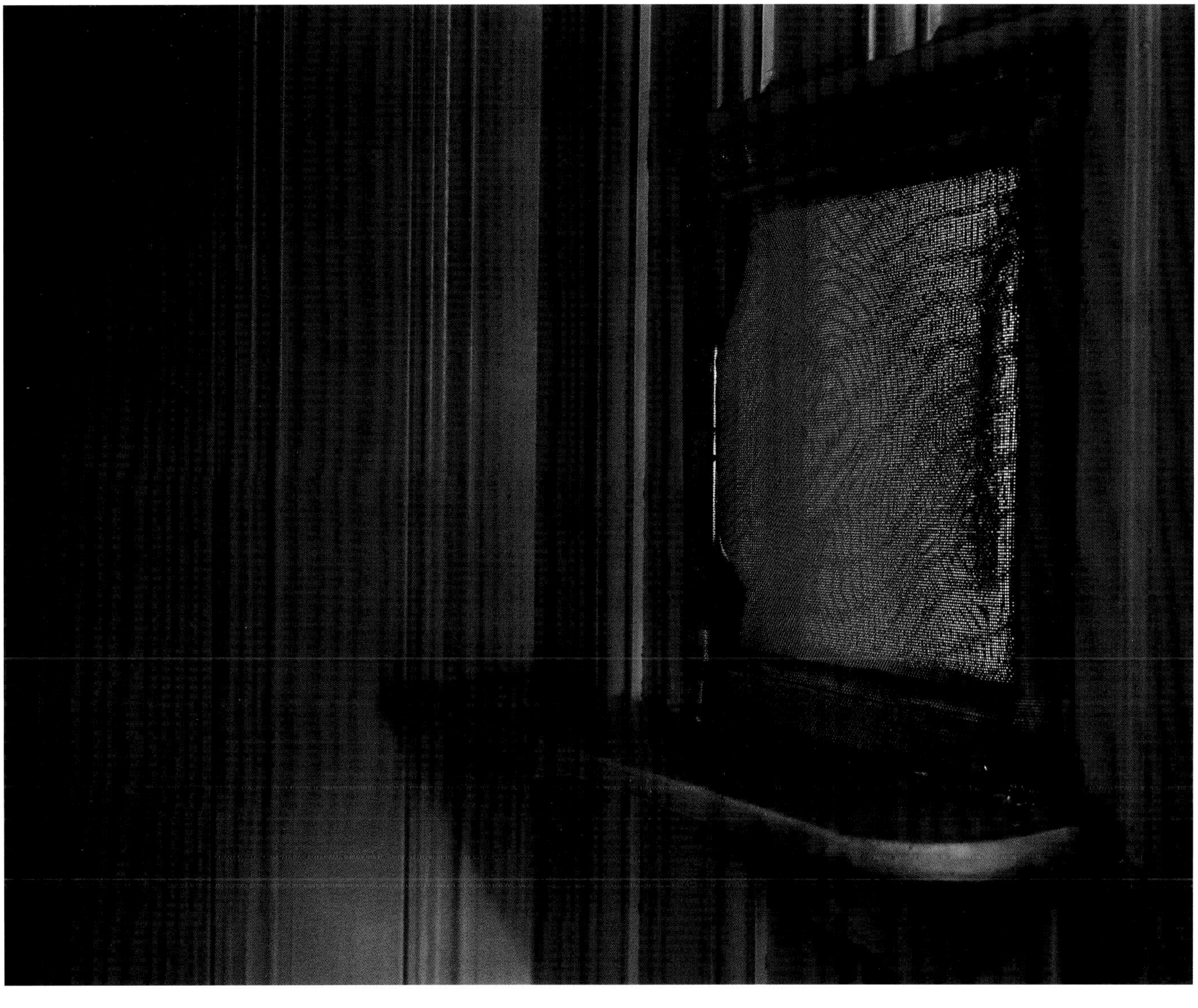

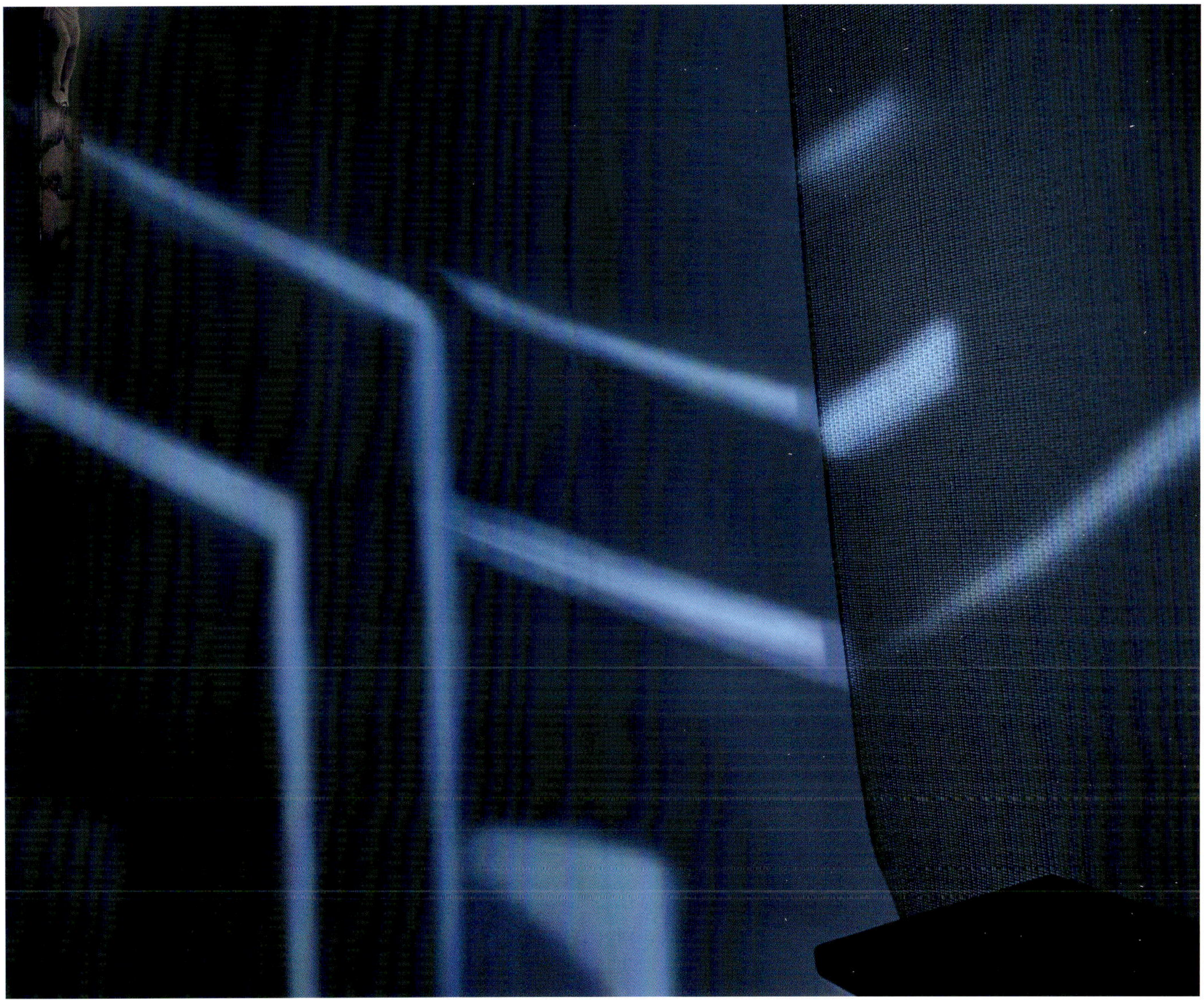

5.

Saint Raphael
Corpus Christi
Our Lady of Angels
Saint Peter
Our Lady of Mount Carmel
Holy Cross
Saint Elizabeth Ann Seton
Saint Barbara

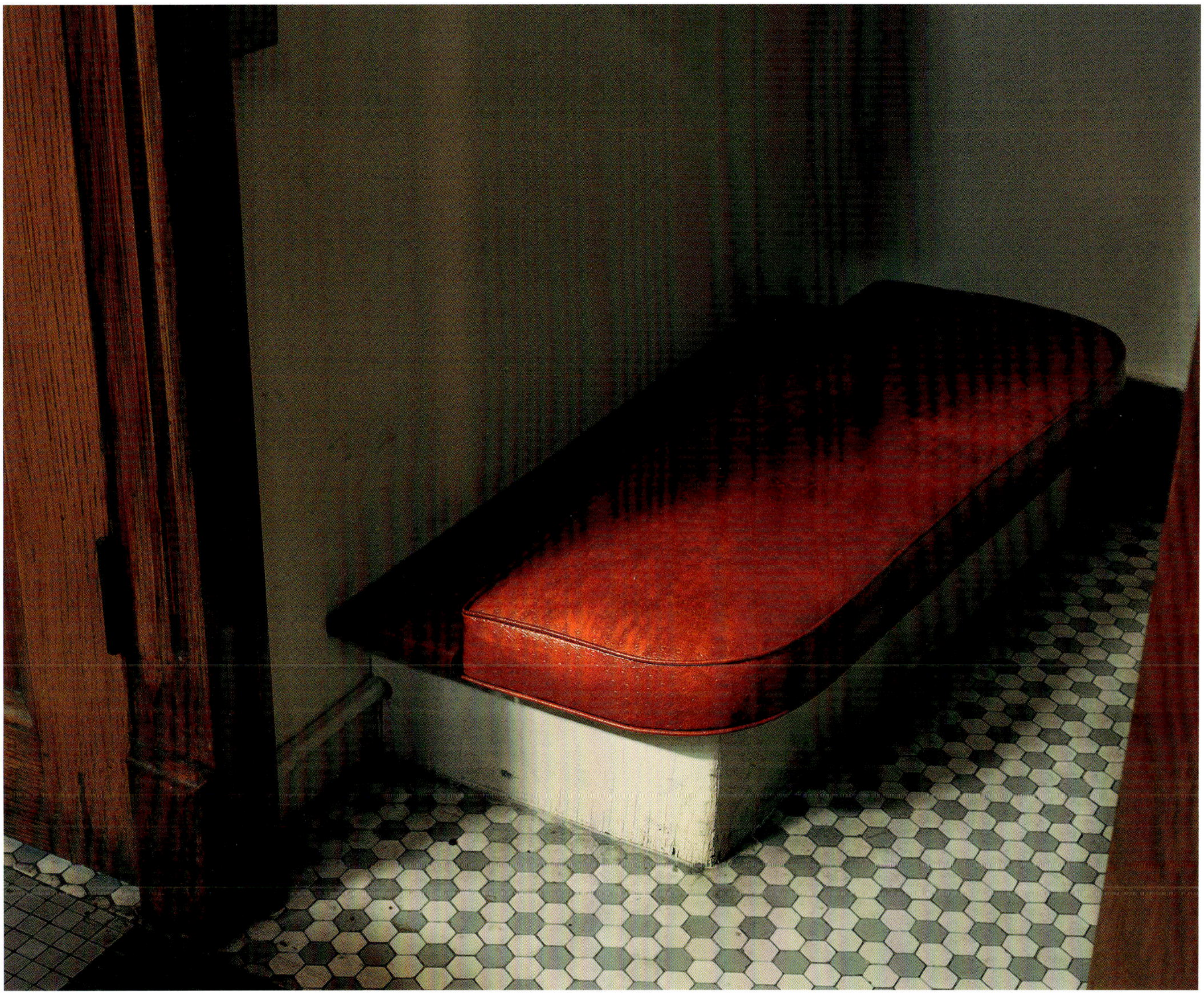

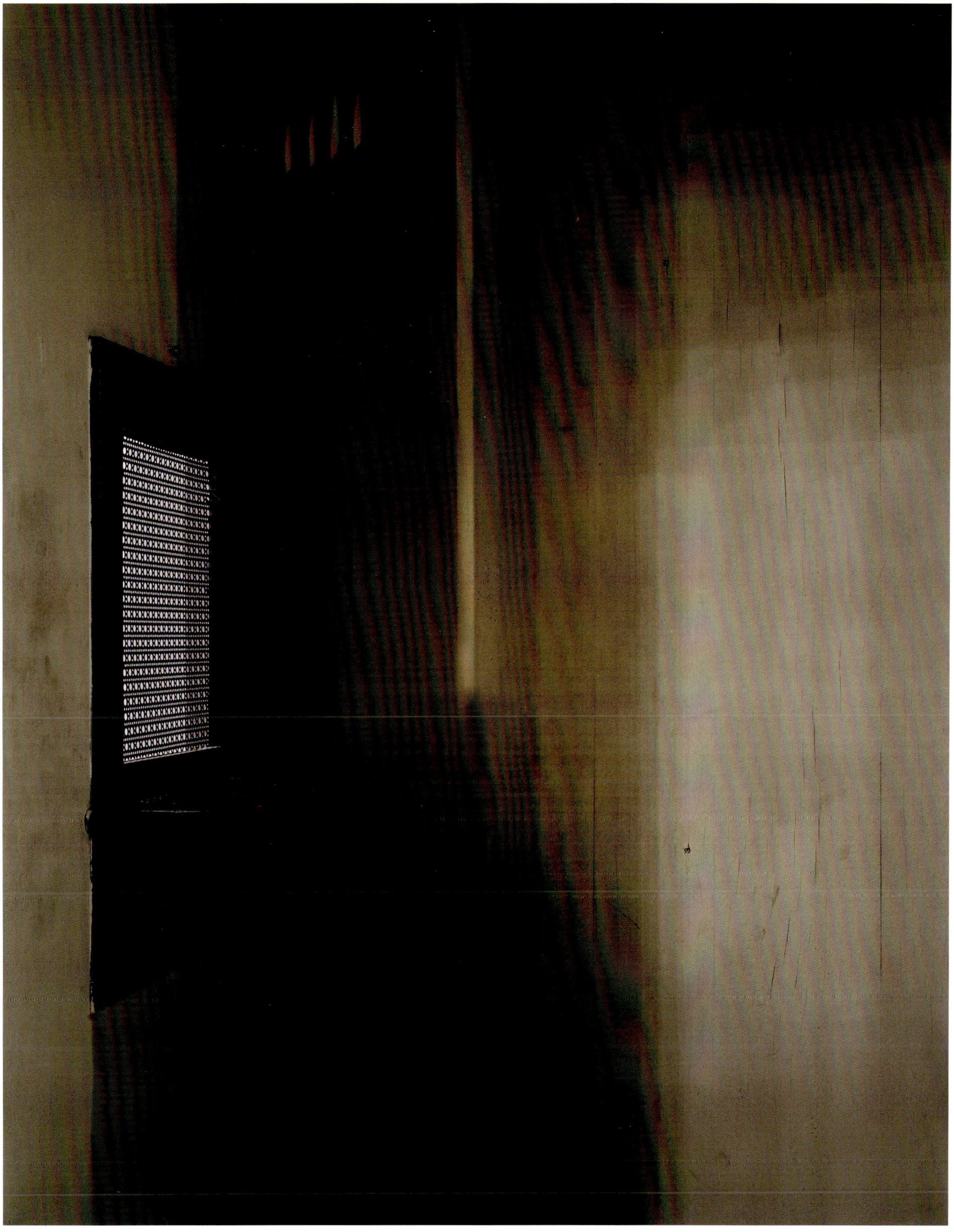

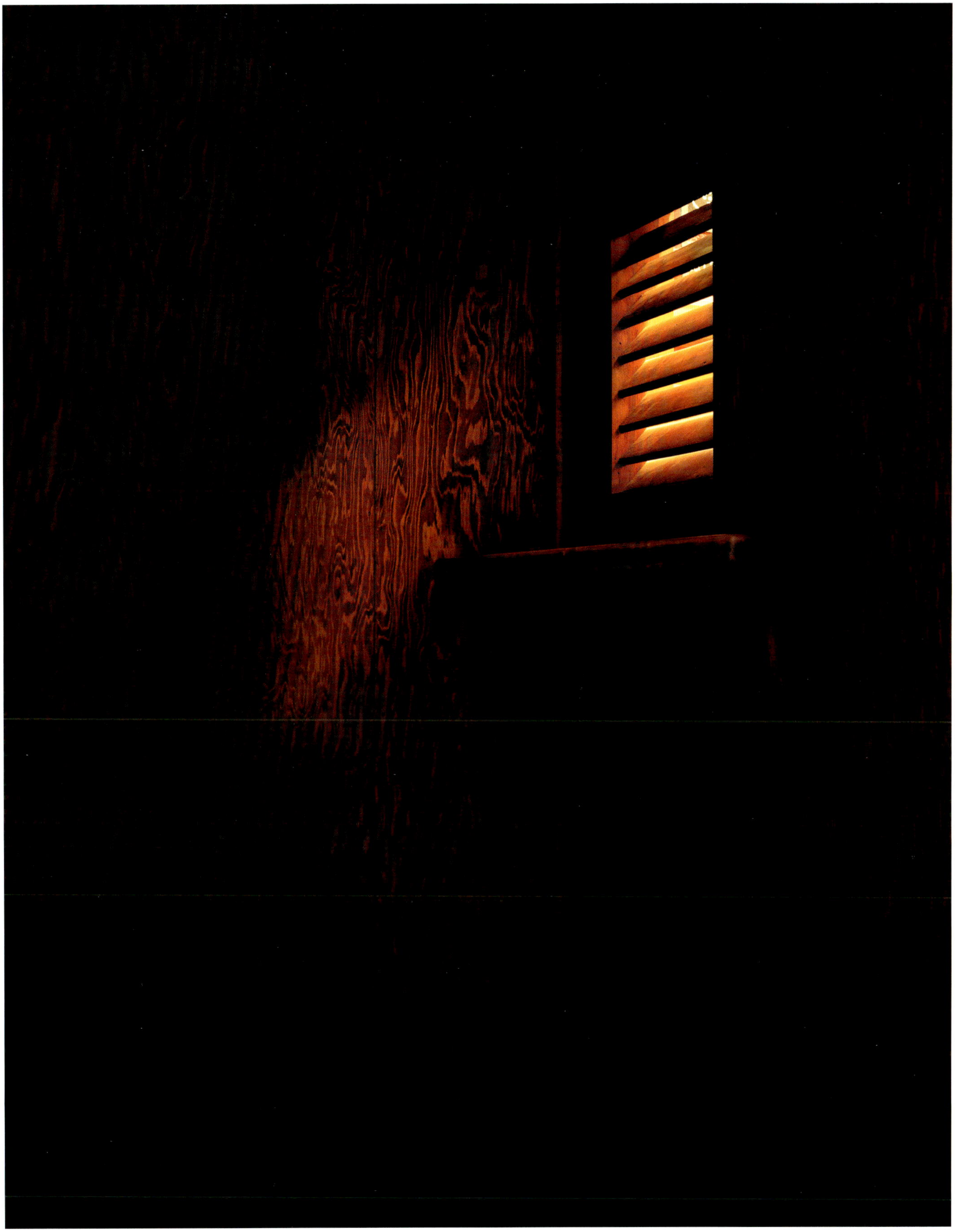

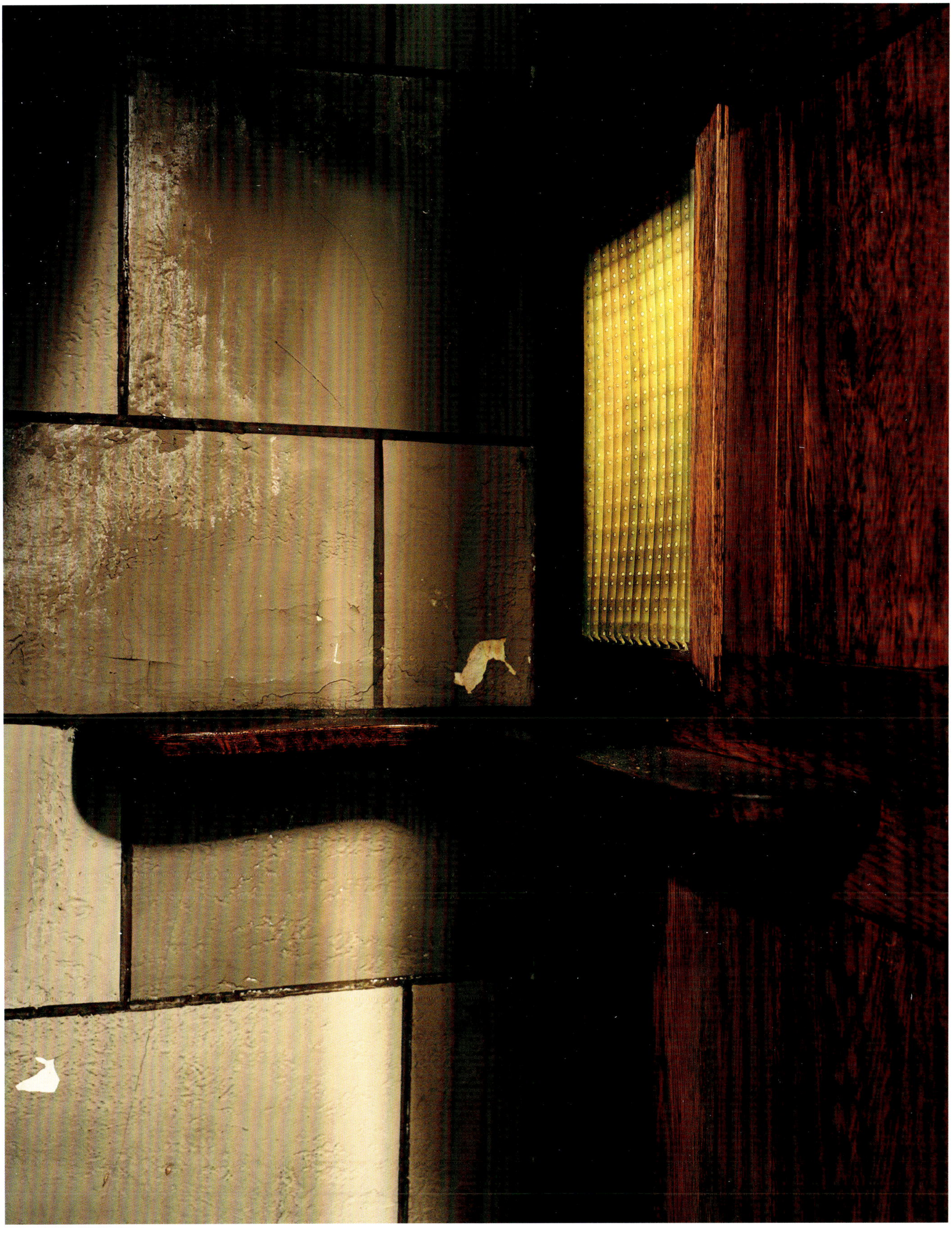

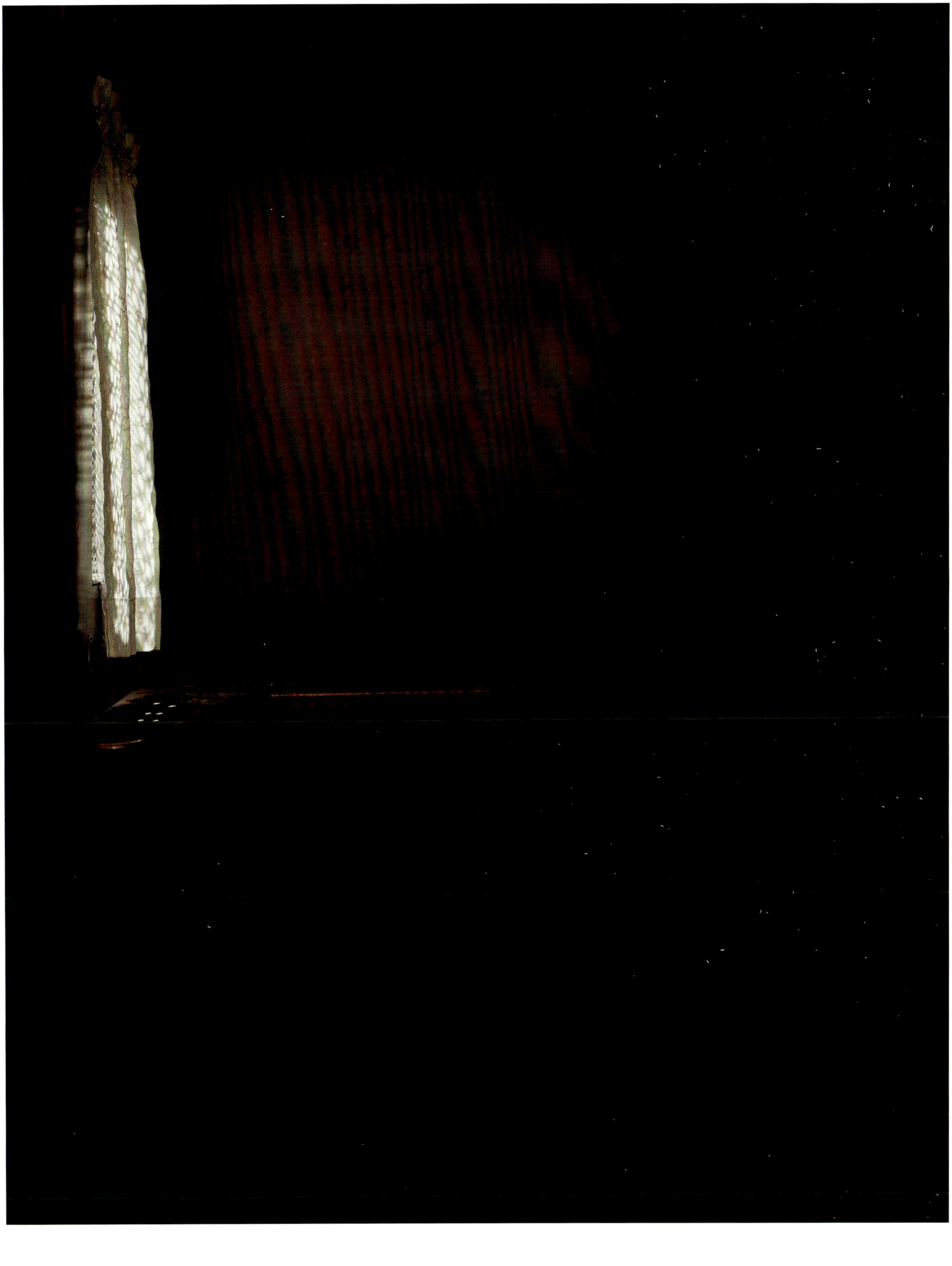

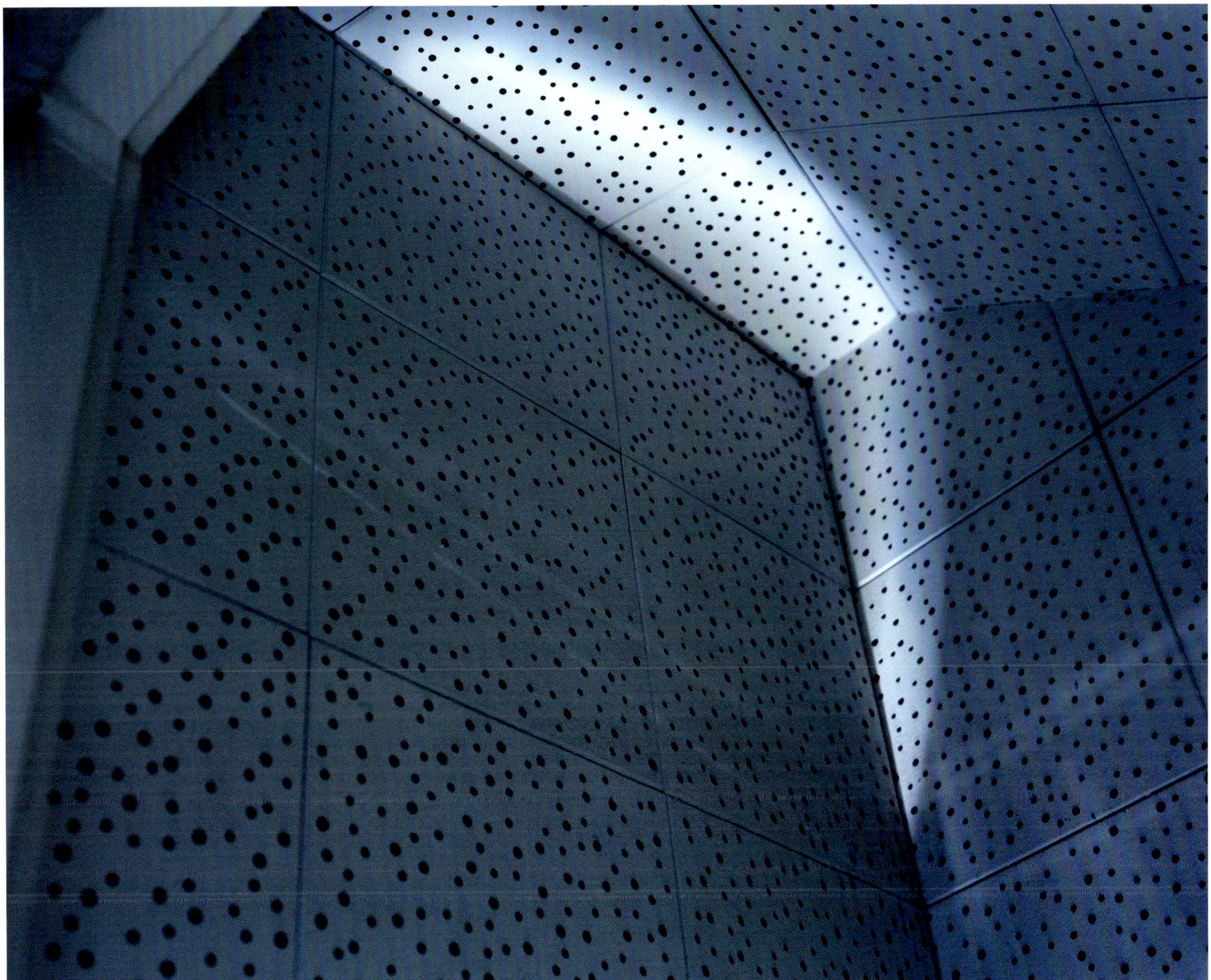

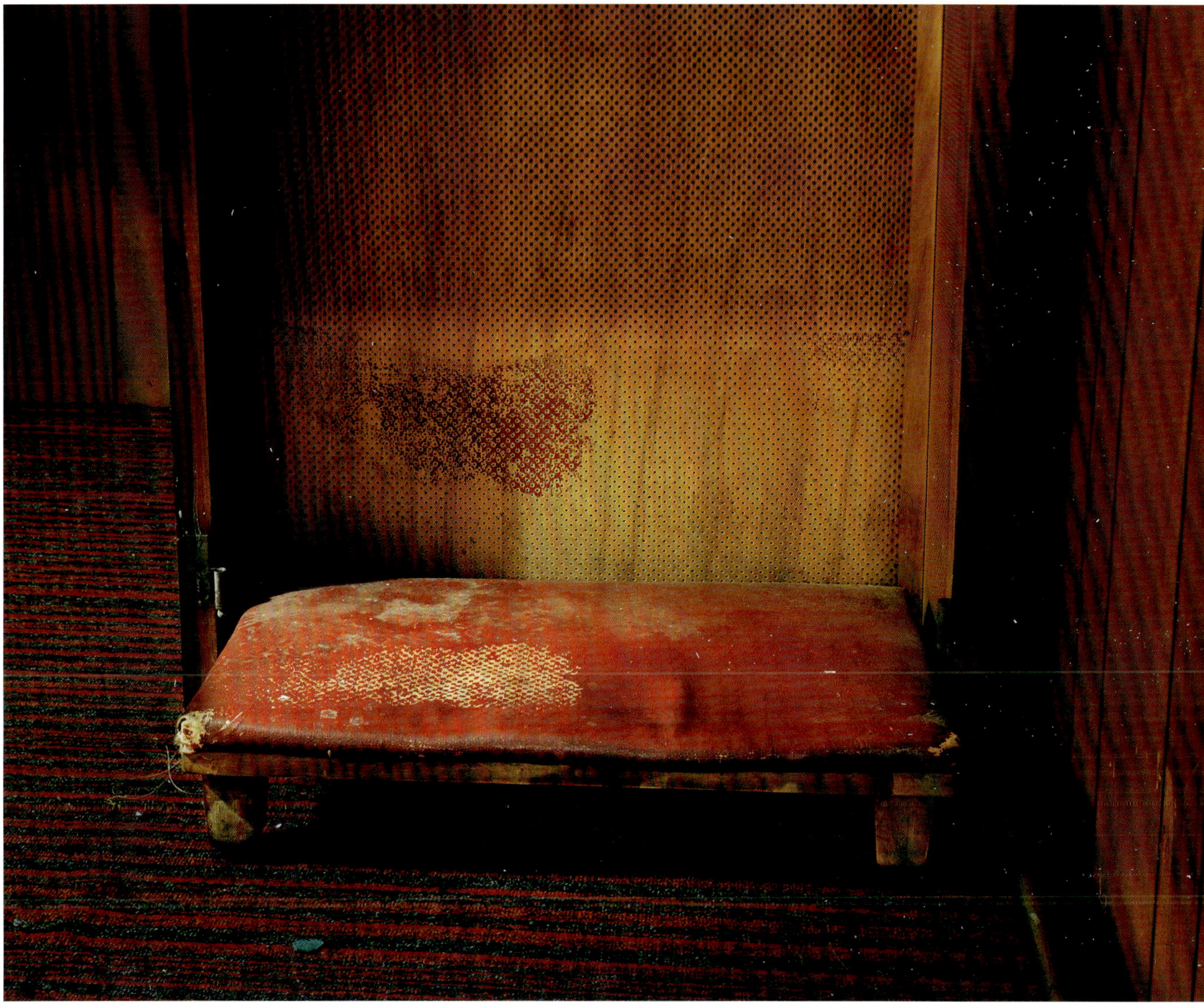

Reconciliation
Kirstin Valdez Quade

Forgive me, Father, for I have sinned. *It's been seven years since my last confession.* Eight months, no, nine. *One week.* I fought with my brother, three times. I punched him in the arm, but only once. *Forgive me, Father.* I cheated on my wife, Father. In the Radisson in Nashville. But the lady hit on me, and I was drunk and tired, and Susan can be so hard. *Forgive me, Father.* I stepped on my husband's toothbrush, really ground the bristles into the tiles, then put it back in the cup, and went to make his favorite peanut curry. *I screamed at a woman in a Honda on Speedway, Father. Screamed horrible things. So much*

hurt in the world, and I added more. I thought my life would be different. Why isn't it different? I feel despair, Father. I have pills. I have a blade. *I don't think I sin that bad. Just normal sins. Like, human sins. Listen to these sins. Do I sin that bad?* Where is God? Why can't I find Him? *I don't belong to this parish, Father. I just confess here. I don't want to be shaking the hand after Mass of the man who's heard all I have to say. I am sorry, Father, so sorry, heartily sorry.* I don't know what good this does, Father. But I still come back every Saturday. Forgive me, Father. *I'm in love and I don't think it's a sin, it doesn't feel like a sin, it feels like love, like goodness, like every beautiful thing He created.* For I have sinned. *We were partying and drunk*

and I didn't take the picture, someone else did, but I passed it along, and now I feel so bad, I know it was wrong, but it's out there, being passed and passed and passed and I don't know how to stop it and I'm so afraid to see her at school on Monday. For I have sinned. *I saw need and looked the other way. I saw need again and looked away again.* I don't always know what to believe, Father. *Forgive me, Father.* I envy, Father. I want. I need. I firmly resolve.

With immense gratitude:

The Massachusetts Cultural Council, Berkshire Taconic Artist's Resource Trust Fund

Alexa Becker, Sylvia Ballhause, Erik Clewe, Klaus Kehrer and everyone at Kehrer Verlag, Kirstin Valdez Quade, Jessica Green and Tom Griffiths at Everything Studio, Regina Schrambling, Robin Kelsey and Sara St. Antoine

Barbara Bosworth, Michael Cardinali, Anna Collette, Matthew Connors, Diane Cook, John Paul Doguin, Pictura Gallery, Janne Höltermann, Len Jenshel, Phil Jung, Justin Kimball, Michael Lesy, Joanne Lukitsh, kara lynch, Sandra Matthews, Laura McPhee, Yola Monakhov Stockton, Matthew Monteith, Abelardo Morell, Claudio Nolasco, Galen Palmer, Sara Greenberger Rafferty, Abraham Ravett, Irina Rozovsky, Bob Sacha, Kane Stewart, Stephen Tourlentes, Hope Tucker, Michael Zachary, and all my students at Hampshire College and Massachusetts College of Art and Design

The Churches where I photographed and their parishes

My parents, Marianne and Peter; my sister, Jessie; and all my families: Mandle, Brindisi, McGonagle, Lai

This book is dedicated with love to Audrey and Jude
and to "Aunt" Liz

These photographs were made in Catholic churches throughout the United States.

Proofreading: Regina Schrambling
Design: Everything Studio
Image Processing: Kehrer Design Heidelberg (Erik Clewe)
Production: Kehrer Design Heidelberg (Tom Streicher)

Bibliographic information published by the Deutsche Nationalbibliothek: The Deutsche Nationalbibliothek lists this publication in the Deutsche Nationalbibliografie; detailed bibliographic data is available on the Internet at http://dnb.dnb.de.

Printed and bound in Germany

ISBN 978-3-86828-951-0

Kehrer Heidelberg Berlin
www.kehrerverlag.com